A School Of Champions!

A Study Skills Program
For
Kindergarten-Grade 2

WRITTEN BY
Rosanne Sheritz Sartori

ILLUSTRATED BY
Harry Norcross

A SCHOOL OF CHAMPIONS!

10-DIGIT ISBN: 1-57543-151-3
13-DIGIT ISBN: 978-1-57543-151-2

COPYRIGHT © 2007 MAR✳CO PRODUCTS, INC
Published by mar✳co products, inc.
1443 Old York Road
Warminster, PA 18974
1-800-448-2197
www.marcoproducts.com

PRINTED IN THE U.S.A.

Table Of Contents

Dedication

This book is dedicated to the memory of my father, Milton Sheritz,
who loved books and learning during his long life of 96 years.
It is my wish that all children would share this love.

I also want to thank my husband, Glenn,
who is a constant support and my resident editor!

Introduction

Welcome to *A School Of Champions!* This book includes a comprehensive, sequential curriculum of study skills for students from Kindergarten through Grade 2. The lessons in this curriculum will help students acquire important study habits as they begin their education, giving them the tools they need to succeed in school and later in life.

Children will relate to the puppet, stories, songs, and activities every lesson includes. And they will learn while they're being entertained.

Champ, Clover, and Scout are playful sibling puppies who want to become champions at *The Blue Ribbon School for Dogs.* By including the puppy puppet in your lessons, you will reinforce your students' learning and make the lessons fun and meaningful.

The program for each grade level includes six lessons that focus on appropriate, essential skills. Since every school is different and every student is unique, you may adapt the lessons to fit particular circumstances. If the lessons seem too long or complex for the students at your school, break the lessons into parts, making *your* study skills curriculum last seven, eight, or even nine weeks.

A different song matching original lyrics to a familiar tune is assigned to each grade level. If your students like to sing, feel free to sing the song more frequently than the lesson suggests. If your students don't like to sing, reduce the suggested singing to a minimum.

You may celebrate each level's final awards ceremony as a separate and elaborate occasion or, as this curriculum suggests, distribute certificates at the end of the final lesson.

Make this curriculum your own! Adapt it to fit your students' needs and your taste. These lessons present important skills that will help your students find success in school and later in life. Enjoy the lessons and help your students become *A School Of Champions!*

Rosanne Sheritz Sartori

Pre/Post Test
FOR KINDERGARTEN

Prior to and after teaching *A School Of Champions!,* ask your students to answer the questions in **bold** with a *thumbs-up* for *yes* and a *thumbs-down* for *no.* Do this exercise as a group if a general classroom comparison is desired or question each student individually and record each score. (*Optional*: The questions beneath the questions in bold may be used to supplement the *Post Test.*)

Compare the students' answers prior to and after presenting *A School Of Champions!*

 Your job at this school is *being a teacher.* Yes or No? (1 point)

What is your job at our school? (1 point)

 The first rule of being a champion student is to try once or twice to do a new thing. Yes or No? (1 point)

When you are taught something new, which *Paw #1* rule will help you learn to do it? (1 point)

 Your ears are the only part of your body that do the work of *listening.* Yes or No? (1 point)

What is one thing you can do to show your teacher that you are following the *Paw #2* rule and being a good listener? (1 point)

 You will remember more of the teacher's directions if you pretend you have a tape recorder in your head and repeat the directions to yourself. Yes or No? (1 point)

What trick can you use to remember the teacher's directions? (1 point)

 You should play first, then do your work. Yes or No? (1 point)

What is the *Paw #3* rule about working and playing? (1 point)

 Knowing how to work in groups is important in school. Yes or No? (1 point)

Why is it important to be able to work with other children in a small group? (1 point)

 To get along in a group, it's important to be able to take turns. Yes or No? (1 point)

What is one thing you can do to get along in a small group? (1 point)

Pre/Post Test
ANSWERS FOR KINDERGARTEN
(7 POINTS POSSIBLE)

 No
(Acceptable answers include: My job at school is *being a student* or *pupil.* My job at school is *to work and learn.)*

 No
(Acceptable answers include: Keep trying until you can do it. Don't give up. Have a good attitude.)

 No
(Acceptable answers include: I must also keep my body still. I must look at the teacher. I must think about what the teacher is saying.)

 Yes
(Acceptable answers include: I can repeat the directions in my head. I can pretend I have a tape recorder in my head. I can hold my body still. I can watch the teacher. I can think about what the teacher is saying.)

 Yes
(Acceptable answers include: You must finish your work before you play. Don't play when it's time to work.)

 Yes
(Acceptable answers include: I'm in a lot of groups. I'm part of a group at school. It's nice to get along. More work gets done in a group. It's more fun to work together than to work alone.)

 Yes
(Acceptable answers include: I can take turns. I can share. I can play fair. I can listen to others. I can be nice to others. I can use good manners.)

Pre/Post Test
DIRECTIONS FOR GRADE 1

Call on students individually and ask the following questions prior to and following implementation of *A School Of Champions!* Record each child's answers.

Since there is a short practice test at the end of Lesson 6, the post test should be administered soon after the last lesson is presented, but not on the same day. (If the students question why they must take two tests, explain that the test in Lesson 6 was to practice test-taking skills and that *this* test measures everything they learned from *A School Of Champions!*)

You may award points for answers that indicate that a student understands the question.

Compare the results prior to and after presenting *A School Of Champions!* Measure the improvement by using plus or minus points or by figuring the percentage of difference the program made.

Pre/Post Test
FOR GRADE 1

 What is your job at this school? (1 point)

 What *feeling words* might describe a person who is trying hard to become a champion? (1 point for every appropriate answer)

 What would you do if your teacher taught you something new, but you couldn't do it even after you tried three times? (1 point)

 What is the difference between *hearing* and *listening?* (1 point)

 Besides using your ears, what can you do to be *a good listener?* (1 point for every appropriate answer)

 When listening to your teacher's directions, why is it helpful to pretend you have a small tape recorder in your head? (1 point)

 What does *being organized* mean? (1 point)

 What is one way you can keep your papers organized? (1 point)

 What does it mean to *use time wisely?* (1 point)

 The last thing you should do before you turn in your work is take time to _____. (1 point)

 Why do teachers give tests? (1 point)

 What can you do to help yourself do well on tests? (1 point for each appropriate answer.)

Pre/Post Test
ANSWERS FOR GRADE 1

Answers will vary. The facilitator must listen to the answers and decide whether the student understands the question being asked. Suggested answers include:

 My job is *being a student*. (*Being a pupil* or *to do Grade 1 work* are also acceptable.)

 This person might feel happy, proud, satisfied, etc.

 I would keep trying until I could do it.

 Hearing is done with ears only. *Listening* is a more difficult task in which your brain is working, too.

 To be a good listener, it helps to keep your body still, your eyes on the speaker, and your mind on what the speaker is saying.

 Pretending you have a tape recorder in your head will help you remember directions you have heard.

 Being organized means having a place for everything and putting everything back in its place. It also means having a system of doing things and doing things the same way every time.

 Using folders is a great way to organize papers. Answers that include *knowing where to put your papers* are also acceptable.

 Using time wisely means *using your time the best way you can*. Don't work too fast or too slowly. Don't waste time.

 Use some time to check your work before you turn it in.

 Teachers give tests to find out how much students have learned and how much they know.

 Answers might include: *having a good attitude (picturing success), taking deep breaths, eating a good breakfast, getting enough sleep the night before, being neat, doing your own work.*

DIRECTIONS FOR GRADE 2

You may give this test orally. You may give it as a written test if you're confident of the second-graders' ability to read and write. Because this ability often varies among students in Grade 2, it is recommended that the facilitator or a helper administer this test orally and record each student's answers.

If an adult is recording students' answers, call on each student individually and ask the following questions prior to and following implementation of *A School Of Champions!*

Since there is a short practice test at the end of Lesson 6, this test should be administered soon after the last lesson is presented, but not on the same day. (If the students question why they must take two tests, explain that the test in Lesson 6 was used to practice test-taking skills and *this* test measures everything they learned from *A School Of Champions!)*

You should award points for answers that indicate that a student understands the question.

Compare the results prior to and after presenting *A School Of Champions!* Measure the improvement by using plus or minus points or by figuring the percentage of difference the program made.

Pre/Post Test
FOR GRADE 2

 1. What is your job this year in school? (1 point)

 2. To help you set a long-term goal, what picture should you keep in your head? (1 point)

 3. Your behavior and the effort you make in Grade 2 every day will affect the success you have in the future. Why? (1 point)

 4. Why wouldn't a champion student want to play during work time? (1 point)

 5. Besides using your ears, what can you do to be *a good listener?* (1 point for every appropriate answer)

 6. When listening to your teacher's directions, why is it helpful to pretend you have a small tape recorder in your head? (1 point)

 7. If your desk is organized, you will never have to clean it out again. Why is this true? (1 point)

 8. What is one good way to organize your papers? (1 point)

 9. How can a person organize his or her time? (1 point)

 10. What does the word *proofread* mean? (1 point)

 11. Proofreading your papers before you turn them in will help you get a better grade. Why is this true? (1 point)

 12. What types of mistakes should you look for when you proofread your papers? (1 point for each appropriate answer)

 13. Why is it important to read all the directions for an assignment? (1 point)

 14. Why is it helpful to look over an assignment before you begin to work? (1 point)

 15. Why do teachers give tests? (1 point)

 16. How can you change *nervousness* about an upcoming test to *confident energy?* (1 point)

 17. What can you do at home to help you do better on tests at school? (1 point for each appropriate answer)

 18. When you are trying to learn spelling words or other new facts, what is a good way to study? (1 point)

ANSWERS FOR GRADE 2

Answers will vary. The facilitator must listen to the answers and decide whether the student understands the question being asked. Suggested answers include:

1. My job is *to be a student* or *pupil*. My job is *to learn Grade 2 material*. My job is *to listen and learn*.

2. I could set a long-term goal by trying to picture what kind of adult I want to be and how I want to feel about myself.

3. My behavior and effort in Grade 2 will affect my future, because I should be learning things every day that I will need to be successful. If I'm playing around or not trying hard, I might not learn something I'll need to know later.

4. A champion student wants to be a winner and tries to do his or her best every day. A champion student would not want to play during work time, because he or she is trying hard to learn.

5. Besides using his or her ears, a good listener must keep his or her body still, look at the person who is speaking, and think about what that person is saying. Pretending to have a tape recorder in your head is also a good thing to do.

6. It is helpful to pretend you have a tape recorder in your head so you can "hear" the teacher's directions more than once. You can repeat the words before you forget them.

7. If I organize my desk, then everything has a place. To keep my desk organized, I always put things back in the right place.

8. Answers might include: *using folders, putting papers in the appropriate places, using book bags, etc.*

9. A person can organize his/her time by making a schedule and making sure to leave time for important things like homework.

10. *Proofread* is another word for checking your work.

🐾 If I proofread my papers, I will probably find mistakes I didn't know I made. If I find mistakes, I can fix them.

🐾 The types of mistakes I should look for might include: *capital letters, punctuation, misspelled words, unfinished problems or missing or incorrect answers, not having written what I thought I wrote.*

🐾 Reading directions is always important, because directions may tell me to do something new or different than I am used to doing. The directions may tell me which questions to answer and how to answer them.

🐾 If I look over the whole assignment before I begin, there will be no surprises. I will be able to see which questions might take more time. If there is something I don't understand, I can ask the teacher at the beginning of our work time.

🐾 Teachers give tests to find out how much I have learned, how much I already know, and how much I still need to learn.

🐾 Taking deep breaths and picturing myself doing well will help my *nervousness* become *energy.* If I am prepared for the test, I will be less nervous and more confident.

🐾 Some things I can do at home to do better on tests at school might include: *eating breakfast, getting a good night's sleep, studying for the test, and doing all my assigned work.*

🐾 When I study, I should be doing something to keep my mind on what I'm trying to learn. Writing something over and over won't help if I'm not thinking about the information.

ASCA STANDARDS

A School Of Champions! will help students in Kindergarten through Grade 2 meet the goals of the American School Counselor Association (ASCA) National Standards for Students as listed below:

Academic Development

Standard A: Students will acquire the attitudes, knowledge and skills that contribute to effective learning in school and across the life span.

A:A1   Improve Academic Self-concept
  A:A1.1   Articulate feelings of competence and confidence as learners
  A:A1.2   Display a positive interest in learning
  A:A1.3   Take pride in work and achievement
  A:A1.4   Accept mistakes as essential to the learning process
  A:A1.5   Identify attitudes and behaviors that lead to successful learning

A:A2   Acquire Skills for Improving Learning
  A:A2.1   Apply time-management and task-management skills
  A:A2.2   Demonstrate how effort and persistence positively influence learning

A:A3   Achieve School Success
  A:A3.1   Take responsibility for their actions
  A:A3.2   Demonstrate the ability to work independently, as well as the ability to work cooperatively with other students
  A:A3.4   Demonstrate dependability, productivity and initiative
  A:A3.5   Share knowledge

Standard B: Students will complete school with the academic preparation essential to choose from a wide range of substantial post-secondary options, including college.

A:B1   Improve Learning
  A:B1.1   Demonstrate the motivation to achieve individual potential
  A:B1.3   Apply the study skills necessary for academic success at each level
  A:B1.5   Organize and apply academic information from a variety of sources
  A:B1.7   Become a self-directed and independent learner

A:B2   Plan to Achieve Goals
  A:B2.1   Establish challenging academic goals in elementary, middle/jr. high and high school
  A:B2.6   Understand the relationship between classroom performance and success in school

Standard C: Students will understand the relationship of academics to the world of work and to life at home and in the community.

A:C1   Relate School to Life Experiences
  A:C1.4   Demonstrate an understanding of the value of lifelong learning as essential to seeking, obtaining and maintaining life goals
  A:C1.6   Understand how school success and academic achievement enhance future career and vocational opportunities

A School Of Champions!

Kindergarten

A School Of Champions!
Kindergarten
(Sung to *The Wheels On The Bus*)

We are the champions at our school,
At our school, at our school!
We are the champions at our school!
We know how to ~~win~~! learn!

We're at school to work and learn,
Work and learn, work and learn!
We're at school to work and learn!
We know how to ~~win~~! learn!

We can do things when we try,
When we try, when we try!
We can do things when we try!
We know how to ~~win~~! learn!

So we'll try hard and never give up,
Never give up, never give up!
We'll try hard and never give up!
We know how to ~~win~~! learn!

20

Goal:

This lesson is an introduction to *A School Of Champions!* for Kindergarten students. The students will learn that each of them now has an important job called *being a student*. This lesson will also motivate the students to want to learn more about becoming champion students.

Materials Needed:

For the leader:
☐ Dog puppet or 4-legged stuffed toy named *Champ*
☐ Paper bag
☐ *A School Of Champions! Kindergarten* song (optional, page 20)

For each student:
☐ 1 piece of 11" x 18" construction paper
☐ Crayons

Presentation Preparation:

Place the puppet/toy dog in the bag. Make sure each student has crayons. Gather the other necessary materials.

Note: In presenting this lesson and the rest of this program's lessons for Kindergarten, it is recommended that you sit in a low chair and that the students sit on the floor in front of you.

Lesson:

INTRODUCTION 1: (You may use this introduction if this is your first lesson of the school year in this classroom. If you have been in this classroom previously, skip to Introduction 2, page 22.)

Introduce the lesson by saying:

> **Hello, boys and girls! My name is _____. Let me hear you say my name together.**

After the children have said your name, continue the lesson by saying:

Good! I want you to remember my name, because I will be coming to your classroom a lot this year. Like many other adults, I have a job at this school. My job is to help children learn and do well in school.

I want to see if you know about some of the jobs at our school.

Do you know what the principal's job is? (To run the school or be the boss)

A person called a *secretary* **works in the office. What is the secretary's job?** (To answer phones, write letters, and help the principal)

What is the job of the school nurse? (To help kids when they are sick or get hurt at school)

What is your teacher's job? (To teach us all the things we will learn in Kindergarten)

If you wish to call attention to other jobs around the school, continue naming other school personnel.

Then explain:

I am the school counselor. I visit all the classrooms in this school and teach lessons that help children do well in school and in other parts of their lives. During my lessons this year, I'll be talking about feelings, friends, how to behave, and how to do well in school.

Sometimes I'll come to your classroom. And sometimes I might invite children to come to my room to talk. You'll see me many times this year, and I hope I'll get to know each of you very well.

Did you know that *YOU* **have a job at this school, too? Who can tell me the name of the job each of you has at this school?** (Children who go to school are called students. Sometimes they are called pupils.)

Yes, it's true! We all have jobs at _____ School, and your job is very special!

INTRODUCTION 2: (Use this introduction if this is not your first lesson of the year in this classroom.)

Hello, boys and girls! Raise your hand if you remember my name. (Ask a student to tell the class your name.)

Who remembers what my job is at this school? (School counselor or whatever the title of your job is)

What is (<u>INSERT TEACHER'S NAME</u>) job at this school? (To teach us everything we need to learn in Kindergarten.)

Great! And what is *your* job at this school? (Student)

Yes, it's true! We *all* have jobs at _____School, and your job is very special.

DISCUSSION: Whether you used Introduction 1 or 2, continue the lesson by saying:

Congratulations on having an important job! Being a Kindergarten student at _____ School is important ... just like being the principal or the nurse or the teacher or the secretary or the counselor. We *all* have special things to do at this school.

As a Kindergarten student, what do you think you will be doing each day at school? (Lead the students to an appropriate answer: A Kindergarten student's job is to work and learn.)

Whenever you have a job, it's important to do your best. I try every day to be the best counselor I can be. Raise your hand if you feel it's important to do your best in school every day.

ACTIVITY: (A show of hands may be used, but it's recommended that the students stand to answer the following questions. This will give them an opportunity to move.)

Conduct the activity by saying:

Please stand if you would like to be a *good* student.

That's wonderful! Now please sit down.

Please stand if would like to be *a great* student.

That's marvelous! Now please sit down.

Please stand if you would like to be a *champion* student!

I am *SO* happy! Now please sit down.

DISCUSSION:

When the children are settled, continue the lesson by asking:

What does the word *champion* mean? (A champion is a winner.)

If a champion is a winner, what is a *champion student?* (A champion student is a student who is a winner in school.)

What do you think you would have to do to be a champion student? (You would have to try to do your best in school every day.)

Just think … if everyone in this school tried to be a champion student, we could have *A School Of Champions!* If you think that would be great, make a thumbs-up sign.

I want you to meet a special friend of mine who also wants to be a champion student. Here he is! (Take Champ out of the bag.)

This is my friend Champ! (Look at the puppet/toy.)

Champ, say *hi* to the boys and girls. (Have Champ bark once.)

Champ wants to learn all about becoming a champion, too. Don't you, Champ? (Have Champ bark once.)

I will be visiting your classroom to teach you some rules that will help you become champion students. Since Champ wants to learn, too, I'll bring him with me each time I come. (Have Champ bark once.)

I will teach you four rules (Hold up four fingers for emphasis.) **that will help you become champions.**

Look thoughtful for a moment, then say:

Four rules … four rules … hmmm … four is the number of paws Champ has! I will teach you one rule for each of Champ's paws. (Count Champ's paws out loud.)

1, 2, 3, 4. That's how we'll remember which lesson we're doing. There will be one lesson for each paw.

Next time I come, I'll teach you the lesson that goes with *Paw #1.*

SONG:

Introduce the song by saying:

Let's sing a song about being champions at our school. I will sing the song first. Then I want you to repeat it until you can sing it with me!

Sing the first verse of the song to the children. Then have them sing the verse with you.

A School Of Champions!/Kindergarten
(Sung to *The Wheels on the Bus*)

**We are the champions at our school,
At our school, at our school!
We are the champions at our school!
We know how to win!**
learn

After singing the first verse, say:

Great job! Here is a verse about what you will be doing each day in Kindergarten.

Sing the second verse of the song to the children. Then have them sing the verse with you.

**We're at school to work and learn,
Work and learn, work and learn!
We're at school to work and learn!
We know how to win!**
learn

ACTIVITY:

Introduce the activity by saying:

Each time I come to your classroom to teach a lesson, you will be given an important paper to help you remember the four rules of how to be champion students. I think it would be helpful for everyone to have a special folder to keep those papers together. So I would like each of you to decorate your own folder now.

Give each student a piece of construction paper and have the students take out their crayons. Show the students how to carefully fold the paper in half. Have the students write their names on the folders, helping those who need help. Then have the students decorate their folders. The teacher or counselor may want to write *A School Of Champions!* at the top of each folder. Collect the folders and any other materials that have been distributed to the students.

CONCLUSION:

Conclude the lesson by saying:

Before Champ and I leave, I want to see if you can remember the name of your job at this school. What is your job in school? (Student)

What does a student do each day? (Work and learn)

And what does a champion student do? (A champion student does his/her best every day!)

Champ and I are going to leave your classroom now. But before we go, let's give a silent cheer for the students who want to be part of *A SCHOOL OF CHAMPIONS!* (Pantomime a silent cheer by waving your arms and opening your mouth wide, but not saying anything.)

Then look at Champ and say:

Champ, before we go, do you have anything to say to the students? (Have Champ bark once.)

When Champ and I come back, we will learn the first *Paw rule* to becoming a champion! We'll see you then. 'Bye.

LESSON 2 – KINDERGARTEN
Champions Try Hard!

Goal:

The students will learn that trying hard is the first important rule of becoming a champion student.

Materials Needed:

For the leader:
- ☐ Dog puppet or 4-legged stuffed toy named *Champ*
- ☐ *A School Of Champions! Kindergarten* song (optional, page 20)
- ☐ Sticky note
- ☐ Marker

For each student:
- ☐ *A School Of Champions!* folder that was prepared in Lesson 1
- ☐ *Paw #1* (page 33)
- ☐ Crayons

Presentation Preparation:

Reproduce *Paw #1* for each student. Write *#1* on the sticky note.

Note: To present this lesson, have children sit on the floor, facing your chair. A surface such as an empty chair, desk, or low table should be within reach of your chair.

Lesson:

INTRODUCTION:

Introduce the lesson by saying:

   Hello, boys and girls! (Have Champ bark once to greet the students.)

DISCUSSION:

Ask the following questions:

Who remembers my name? (Let a student answer.)

What is my job? (Counselor)

What is *YOUR* job at school? (Student)

Great! And do you remember what today's lesson is going to be about? (The students are going to be learning rules that will help them become a part of *A School Of Champions!* They will learn one rule for each of Champ's paws. Today, they will learn *Paw #1 rule.*)

Today, we are going to learn the first rule for the first paw! (Place the sticky note with #1 on it on one of Champ's front paws.)

What does it mean to be a *champion student?* (A champion is a winner, and a champion student is a student who works and learns and tries to do his/her best in school every day.)

SONG:

Review the song learned in first session by saying:

Last week, we learned two verses of a song about becoming part of *A School Of Champions!* Let's sing the verses together.

A School Of Champions!/Kindergarten
(Sung to *The Wheels on the Bus*)

We are the champions at our school,
At our school, at our school!
We are the champions at our school!
We know how to win! *learn!*

We're at school to work and learn,
Work and learn, work and learn!
We're at school to work and learn!
We know how to win! *learn!*

When you and the children have finished singing the song, compliment the students by saying:

Great job!

DISCUSSION:

Continue the lesson by saying:

During our last lesson, I told you that Champ wants to be a champion student. Just like all of you. Right, Champ? (Look at Champ and have him bark one time.)

And I told you that we're going to learn four lessons—one for each of Champ's paws—that will help you become champions. (Have Champ bark once.)

Well, let's get going! Today, we'll talk about the first *Paw* to being a champion student. (Point to the sticky note on Champ's front paw.)

But first I want to tell you about a little story about Champ. (Have Champ look at the children and bark once.)

STORY:

Read or tell the following story to the children. As you're reading or telling the story, use the puppet/toy to demonstrate.

Champ really wants to learn to be a champion in school, but he has come to realize that being a champion isn't always easy. Last week, Champ's teacher, Mrs. Beagle, taught the class to roll over. Many of the puppies in Champ's class could roll over very easily. They were happy and laughing and showing each other how much fun it was.

But Champ was having trouble doing this new trick. Each time he tried, he got a good start by lying on his side. (Put Champ on his side on a nearby surface.)

Then he would roll onto his back. (Put Champ on his back.**)**

But that was it. Once Champ was on his back, he'd get stuck. His paws were in the air, and he just couldn't make his body turn to the other side.

"Help!" Champ called to his teacher. When she came running over to see what was going on, Champ said, "I'm stuck!"

Mrs. Beagle helped Champ get back to his feet. (Turn Champ upright again.)

Then Champ said, "I can't roll over. It's too hard."

Mrs. Beagle listened, then answered, "Some of the things I ask you to do might seem hard at first. But you can do them if you keep trying!"

Champ looked sad as he said, "I *can't* do it … and I *did* try hard!"

Mrs. Beagle told Champ that champion students don't give up. They keep trying and trying until they *can* do it! She showed Champ again how to roll over. Then she said, "I'm going to leave you alone to practice. Keep practicing and call me when you're able to roll over."

Champ tried and tried, but he got stuck every time. "I'll never be able to show Mrs. Beagle I can roll over," he said to himself. (Demonstrate Champ getting stuck several times, with his legs in the air.)

Champ felt like giving up, but he didn't want to disappoint his teacher. And he *really* wanted to be able to roll over! So he continued to try and try.

At last, he took a deep breath and pushed hard and… (Demonstrate Champ rolling over completely.)

Champ yelled, "Mrs. Beagle, Mrs. Beagle! I *AM* a champion! I can do it!"

Mrs. Beagle smiled. The rest of the puppies watched as Champ rolled over again and again. The puppies were so happy for Champ that they gave him a big cheer. Do you know how puppies cheer? They bark three times! What do you think Champ's classroom sounded like when all the puppies cheered for him? (Have the children bark to show how the classroom sounded.)

DISCUSSION:

Continue the lesson by asking:

Boys and girls, are there things you can do now that you had trouble learning to do? (Let the students tell stories of things they had difficulty with—tying shoes, riding bikes, playing catch, etc.)

Do you think everything you'll be asked to do in Kindergarten will be easy? (No, there are going to be some hard tasks ahead.)

Then say:

The first rule you must learn to become a part of *A School Of Champions!* is that you must have a good attitude. You have to keep trying and trying, even when things seem hard. Just like Champ! YOU CAN'T GIVE UP!

What if you had given up (USE ONE OF THE EXAMPLES FROM THE PREVIOUS QUESTION. FOR EXAMPLE: TRYING TO RIDE A BIKE)? (You wouldn't have ever learned to do it.)

So my question to you is: Will you try very hard each day? If so, raise one hand.

Even if things seem very hard to do? If so, raise both hands.

What if you try something and can't do it the first time? What will you do? (Lead the students to say the answer out loud together: "Try again!")

What if you can't do it the second time you try? (Lead the students to say the answer out loud together: "Try again!")

What if you can't do it the third time you try? (Lead the students to say the answer out loud together: "Try again!")

Even if you try doing something 10 times and aren't able to do it, what should you do? (Lead the students to say the answer out loud together: "Try again!")

Mrs. Beagle was right when she told Champ that he would be able to do his trick if he didn't stop trying. This rule will work for you, too.

THAT is the first rule to being a champion! So the rule that goes with Champ's first paw is: TRY HARD!

SONG:

Continue the lesson by saying:

Let's sing some new words to our song.

Sing the following song and have the students repeat the words until they have learned them.

A School Of Champions!/Kindergarten
(Sung to *The Wheels on the Bus*)

We can do things when we try,
When we try, when we try!
We can do things when we try!
We know how to win!
learn!

So we'll try hard and never give up,
Never give up, never give up!
We'll try hard and never give up!
We know how to win!
learn!

A School Of Champions! © 2007 Mar*co Products, Inc. 1.800.448.2197

ACTIVITY:

Begin the activity by saying:

> **Because you want to become a part of** *A School Of Champions!* **I believe you'll keep trying even when things seem hard.** *Paw #1* **is a great rule to follow!**
>
> **I want you to remember this important rule, so I'm going to give you a special worksheet with** *Paw #1* **on it.**

Show the students the worksheet with the first *Paw*. Give each student his/her folder, a copy of the worksheet, and crayons. Tell the students to write their names on the worksheets. (If needed, you may help the children write their names on the worksheet or you may write their names on the worksheet ahead of time.) Then tell the students to color their worksheet.

CONCLUSION:

As the students complete the *Paw #1* worksheet, ask each child to restate the rule. Be sure that each student says something like, "I won't give up" or "I will keep trying." Coach a child, if necessary, by asking such questions as, "What will you do if your teacher asks you to do something that seems very hard? Will you give up? How will you learn to do hard things?"

Instruct the students to put their worksheets into their folders. Collect the folders and any other materials that have been distributed to the students.

Conclude the lesson by saying:

> **Champ and I will be back, boys and girls! And next time, we'll teach you the rule that goes with Champ's second paw. It will help make you a part of** *A School Of Champions!* **I will be checking with your teacher to make sure you are following the** *Paw #1 rule* **and that you're trying very hard every day to do what your teacher asks you to do and that you're not giving up.**
>
> **I'm excited that we're going to have** *A School Of Champions!*

Optional: Sing any or all verses of *A School Of Champions!* song.

Paw #1

_____
(NAME)

Will
Try Hard
And
Practice Every Day
And Never Give Up!

Champions Know How To Listen!

Goal:

The students will learn the importance of listening and will learn good listening habits. The students will then be given opportunities to practice listening and following directions.

Materials Needed:

For the leader:
- ☐ Champ puppet/stuffed toy with sticky note #1 on one front paw
- ☐ *A School Of Champions! Kindergarten* song (optional, page 20)
- ☐ Marker
- ☐ Sticky note

For each student:
- ☐ *A School Of Champions!* folder prepared in Lesson 1
- ☐ *Paw #2* (page 41)
- ☐ Crayons

Presentation Preparation:

Reproduce *Paw #2* for each student. Write *#2* on a sticky note and place it on Champ's other front paw.

Lesson:

INTRODUCTION:

Introduce the lesson by saying:

Hello, boys and girls! Champ and I are back to teach you the second *Paw* to becoming a champion student. (Point to Champ's front paw with the #2 sticky note on it.)

REVIEW:

Review the previous lesson by asking:

Who remembers the rule that goes with Champ's first paw? (Always try hard and don't give up, even when things are hard.)

How did you do this week with trying hard? (Give students an opportunity to share stories of success.)

We learned a song about becoming part of *A School Of Champions!* **Let's sing the words we have learned so far.**

Lead the students in singing *A School Of Champions!*

A School Of Champions!/Kindergarten
(Sung to *The Wheels on the Bus*)

We are the champions at our school,
At our school, at our school!
We are the champions at our school!
We know how to win!

We're at school to work and learn,
Work and learn, work and learn!
We're at school to work and learn!
We know how to win!

We can do things when we try,
When we try, when we try!
We can do things when we try!
We know how to win!

So we try hard and never give up,
Never give up, never give up!
We try hard and never give up!
We know how to win!

When you and the children have finished singing the song, say:

Wow, you are great singers!

DISCUSSION AND STORY:

Introduce the story by saying:

Champ is here again, (Have Champ bark once.) **and he and I are ready to teach you the second** *Paw* **to becoming a champion student.** (Point to Champ's paw with the #2 sticky note.)

Let me start by telling you a story about what happened to Champ.

Last Monday, Mrs. Beagle told her class that she was going to teach the puppies another new trick.

Champ was very excited. He started talking with his friends. "What do you think the new trick will be?" Champ asked Randy and Trixie. "Will it be something we'll be able to do right away? Will it be fun? Will it be hard to learn?"

Mrs. Beagle had asked all the puppies to sit down, but Champ didn't hear her. Why do you think Champ didn't hear what Mrs. Beagle said? (He was busy talking.)

Mrs. Beagle walked over to Champ and said, quite loudly, "CHAMP, sit down and stop talking … now!"

Champ was embarrassed that his teacher had to speak to him this way. He said, "I'm sorry, Mrs. Beagle, but I didn't hear you."

Mrs. Beagle then said to the class, "Puppies, I just realized that before I can teach you any more tricks, I must teach you the second *Paw* **to becoming a champion student. Champ helped me realize this."**

Champ looked very happy to be an important helper to his teacher.

Mrs. Beagle told the puppies that the second *Paw* **to becoming a champion student is to know how to listen!**

DISCUSSION AND ACTIVITY:

Continue the lesson by asking:

What is the second *Paw* **you must learn in order to become a champion student?** (You must know how to listen!*)*

Why is knowing how to listen so important? (Much of what we learn comes to us from the words of teachers and other adults. We have to listen in order to learn what teachers and other adults are saying.)

Since knowing how to listen is so important, let's talk about how to do it. Many children think that listening is all about using your ears. But other parts of your body also need to do some work.

What should your body be doing when you are listening? (Your body should be still.)

Then say:

Let's practice: While I count to 3, you may wiggle around. When I say, "FREEZE!" you should immediately become still. OK, ready … 1, 2, 3! (Let the children wiggle for several seconds. Then say clearly, "Freeze!" Do this several more times until the children stop wiggling and are very still.)

Good job! OK, so your body should be still while you're listening. What about your eyes? Where should your eyes be? (Your eyes should be looking at the person who is speaking.)

Yes, your *eyes* help your *ears* listen! When you're looking around at something else, you're not doing a good job of listening.

Let's practice: While I'm counting to 3, I want you to look all around the room. But when I say, "LOOK HERE!" I want all eyes on me. OK, ready … 1, 2, 3! (Let the children look around the room for several seconds. Then say clearly, "Look here!" Practice until all eyes are on you.)

Good job! OK, your body is still and your eyes are on the teacher. What about your mind? What should you be thinking about when you are listening? (Prompt the students by asking the following questions.)

Should you be thinking about recess? (No)

Should you be thinking about what you're going to do when you get home? (No)

What should you be thinking about? (You should be thinking about what the teacher is saying.)

Let me look around and let me see if everyone is listening. (Look at each student carefully.)

Great! I can tell that you're all trying to listen.

ACTIVITY:

Begin the activity by saying:

Your teacher gives directions each day. It's very important to listen so you can follow these directions. Following directions is a big part of learning.

Let's practice: I'm going to give some directions. I want you to be ready to listen. Remember, that means that your body is still, your eyes are on me, and you must be thinking about what I'm saying. Look at me if you're ready to try. (Look at each child carefully.)

Good! It looks like everyone is ready.

Give each direction in one breath. Start with simple directions, then progress to more involved directions. Give the children an opportunity to follow each direction, then praise their ability to listen. Say:

Stand up, turn around one time, and sit down.

Stand up, touch your toes, and sit down.

Stand up, wave at me, and sit down.

Put your hand in the air, put your hand on your head, look at me. (Many students will begin to stand, because the first three examples started with standing. Smile, stop everyone and say, "Wait! You must listen carefully. I didn't say you should stand!")

Pat your head, pat your stomach, smile at me.

Tell the students you're going to give them a really difficult direction. Ask them to raise their hands if they're ready for a challenge. Then say:

Stand up, turn around once, raise your hands in the air, and sit down.

This direction has four parts, so the students may get confused. Give them the following information:

Boys and girls, I have heard some children say, "I'm trying to listen, but I can't remember all that stuff!" I want to teach you a trick that will help you remember. I want you to pretend that you have a small tape recorder in your head.

What does a tape recorder do? (It repeats the words that are taped. If I say, "Good morning!" the tape recorder will say, "Good morning!" if I push the *play* button.)

That's what I want you to do with my words. If I say, "Stand up and turn around one time," I want you to say those words in your heads before you follow the instruction.

Are you ready to try?

Stand up, turn around once, and sit down. (Encourage the students to repeat your words silently. Praise students who are mouthing the directions.)

Are you ready to follow a super-hard direction? (Make sure each child's body is still, his/her eyes are on you, and he/she is thinking about your words.)

Raise your hand, wave at me, stand up, then sit down.

Pat your head, pat your stomach, pat your head, and smile at me! (Encourage the students to repeat the directions silently before they move. Stop anyone who is not taking time to think about the directions.)

Great job! You have now learned the second *Paw* to becoming a champion student!

SONG:

Lead the students in singing *A School Of Champions!* Say:

We have new words for our song. I will start singing, and I want you to join me!

Sing the following verse. Have the students repeat the words until they have learned them.

A School Of Champions!/Kindergarten
(Sung to *The Wheels on the Bus*)

We sit still and listen each day,
Listen each day, listen each day!
We sit still and listen each day!
We know how to win!

After singing this verse, you may lead the children in singing the previously learned verses.

We are the champions at our school,
At our school, at our school!
We are the champions at our school!
We know how to win!

We're at school to work and learn,
Work and learn, work and learn!
We're at school to work and learn!
We know how to win!

We can do things when we try,
When we try, when we try!
We can do things when we try!
We know how to win!

So we try hard and never give up,
Never give up, never give up!
We try hard and never give up!
We know how to win!

When you and the children have finished singing the song, compliment them by saying:

Great job!

CONCLUSION:

Conclude the lesson by saying:

I have a *Paw #2* worksheet for you. Remember: To be part of *A School of Champions* you must know how to _____! (Let the children end the sentence with, "LISTEN!")

Give each student his/her folder, a copy of *Paw #2*, and crayons. Then say:

I want you to color this worksheet and keep it in your folder. When you look at it, I hope it will remind you that a champion student must always _____.
(Again, let the children end the sentence with, " LISTEN!")

Pick Champ up and say:

Champ, I hope you've learned this important lesson. Do you know how to listen?
(Have Champ bark once.)

Collect the folders and any other materials that have been distributed to the students. Thank the students for their participation.

_____
(NAME)

Knows
How To
Listen
And
Sit Still!

REPORT CARD

Math   A+
Listening   A+
Reading   A
Writing   A+

Champions Work During Work Time!

Goal:

The students will learn that there is a time for work and a time for play. They will learn that champions do their work first, then have time for play.

Materials Needed:

For the leader:
- ☐ Champ puppet/stuffed toy with sticky notes #1 and #2 on front paws
- ☐ *A School Of Champions! Kindergarten* song (optional, page 20)
- ☐ Sticky note
- ☐ Marker
- ☐ Bag

For each student:
- ☐ *A School Of Champions!* folder prepared in Lesson 1
- ☐ *Work Before Play* (page 48)
- ☐ *Paw #3* (page 49)
- ☐ Crayons

Presentation Preparation:

Reproduce *Paw #3* and *Work Before Play* for each student. Write *#3* on the sticky note.

Lesson:

INTRODUCTION:

Introduce the lesson by saying:

> **Hello, boys and girls! Champ and I are back to teach you the rule that goes with
> *Paw #3.* The rule we learn today will help you become a part of *A School Of
> Champions!* (Place the #3 sticky note on one of Champ's back paws.)

What is the *Paw #1 rule?* (Point to the paw with sticky note #1. The rule is: Try hard and keep practicing every day–even when things are hard.)

How are you doing with following this rule? Are you all trying hard each day? (Allow a short time for success stories.)

What is the *Paw #2 rule?* (Point to the paw with sticky note #2. The rule is: Sit still and listen every day. Review as much as the class needs–body still, eyes on speaker, mind on what the speaker is saying.)

I think I'll ask your teacher how all of you are doing with following this rule. (If the teacher is in the room, ask how the class is doing. Otherwise, omit this sentence.)

It sounds like you are on the way to becoming part of *A School Of Champions!* Congratulations!

Before we learn the *Paw #3 rule,* let's sing!

SONG:

Lead the students in singing *A School Of Champions!* (Sing as much of the song as desired. If the children like to sing, feel free to sing all the verses learned so far. Otherwise, sing the first and last verses learned.)

A School Of Champions!/Kindergarten
(Sung to *The Wheels on the Bus*)

We are the champions at our school,
At our school, at our school!
We are the champions at our school!
We know how to win!

We're at school to work and learn,
Work and learn, work and learn!
We're at school to work and learn!
We know how to win!

We can do things when we try,
When we try, when we try!
We can do things when we try!
We know how to win!

So we try hard and never give up,
Never give up, never give up!
We try hard and never give up!
We know how to win!

We sit still and listen each day,
Listen each day, listen each day!
We sit still and listen each day!
We know how to win!

Following directions helps us learn,
Helps us learn, helps us learn!
Following directions helps us learn!
We know how to win!

When you and the children have finished singing the song, compliment the students by saying:

Wow, you are great singers!

STORY:

Introduce the story by asking:

Are you ready to learn the rule that goes with Champ's third paw? (Point to the paw that is labeled #3 and have Champ bark one time.)

Before I tell you the rule, I want to tell you a little more about Champ.

Champ loves to go to school. How many of you feel the same way? (Hopefully, all hands will be raised.)

But Champ also likes to play. How many of you like to play? (All hands will probably be raised.)

The problem is that Champ sometimes gets mixed up about this.

One day, Mrs. Beagle was teaching Champ's class the importance of staying out of the street. The puppies were good listeners as she told them about the dangers of cars on the road.

Then Mrs. Beagle told the class that she was going to divide the puppies into three groups. She wanted each group to make up a rule about street safety.

Champ was put in the same group as his best friends, Trixie and Jake. Champ was sitting next to Trixie, and he noticed that her tail was curled up right next to him.

Even though the puppies were supposed to be working, Champ couldn't help himself. He gave Trixie's tail a little tug. Trixie didn't like that, so she ran around and tried to pull Champ's tail. Then Jake joined in the fun. The next thing you know, Champ, Trixie, and Jake were running around in circles, chasing one another's tails.

"Freeze!" shouted Mrs. Beagle. Champ, Trixie, and Jake stopped at once. It was then that Mrs. Beagle told the class that the students had to learn a new rule if they wanted to be champion students.

Mrs. Beagle gathered all the puppies around her and said, "Boys and girls, if you want to become part of *A School Of Champions!* there is another rule I need to teach you: Work comes before play. During work time, you should work. During play time, you may play. But don't play during work time!

After teaching this rule to the class, Mrs. Beagle put the puppies in small groups and reminded them that each group was supposed to make up a rule about street safety. Champ's group settled down to work and came up with a great rule. The rule was: Don't PLAY in the street!

DISCUSSION:

Continue the lesson by saying:

Boys and girls, the rule Mrs. Beagle taught Champ's class is the rule that goes with *Paw #3.*

Here is the rule: Work comes before play. During work time, you should work! During play time, you may play! But don't play during work time!

It can be as hard for children in Kindergarten to remember this rule as it is for puppies. But if you want to be part of *A School Of Champions!* you must try to follow this important rule.

It's my guess that the adults in your life try to follow this rule. Your families all have work to do. And when they have finished working, they stop to have fun, relax, and play. This is an important rule in school and in life.

SONG:

Teach the children the next verse of the *A School Of Champions!* song. Say:

Let's learn and sing another verse of our song!

Sing the following verse and have the students repeat the words until they have learned them.

A School Of Champions!/Kindergarten
(Sung to *The Wheels on the Bus*)

Work comes first and then we play,
Work then play, work then play!
Work comes first and then we play!
We know how to ~~win~~! learn

ACTIVITY 1:

Begin the activity by saying:

We're going to practice the rule we have just learned. We're going to do some work right now. I have a worksheet that will let me see how well you can follow directions. This is work time! When you have finished, we'll play a game. But remember: Work comes first, then play.

Give each student his/her folder and crayons. Then say:

You're going to have to listen carefully and get the "tape recorders in your brains" ready to repeat my directions. You'll need three crayons: red, green, and blue.

Repeat the directions, if necessary, and give the students time to take the three crayons out of their crayon box.

Give each student a copy of *Work Before Play*. As you're giving the directions, stop periodically to praise the students for their effort. Give compliments such as, "I can tell that everyone is working hard and really knows how to follow the work rule. You are champions!"

Give the following directions:

Paw #1   **With your blue crayon, draw a circle in the paw print.**

Paw #2   **With your red crayon, draw a smiling face in the paw print.**

Paw #3   **With your green crayon, draw a straight line from one corner of the paw print to the other corner.**

Paw #4   **With your red crayon, draw a squiggly, jiggly line from one corner of the paw print to the other corner.**

Paw #5   **With your blue crayon, draw a small box in the middle of this paw print.**

Paw #6   **Use all 3 colors to draw a rainbow in the last paw print.**

Then compliment the children by saying:

You all did a great job at work! Now that we have finished working, it's play time! Let's play a game!

ACTIVITY 2:

Lead the students in any game that is a class favorite or present the following activity. To present the following activity, say:

Let's form a circle. Listen carefully and do what I say. (Say the following sentences slowly enough so students can follow the directions and not trip over each other.)

> **Stretch to the sky, sky, sky,**
> **now to the floor, floor, floor!**
> **Join hands and walk to the right, right, right!**
> **Stop! And listen some more, more, more!**
>
> **Put your hands on your head, head, head,**
> **and now on your knees, knees, knees!**
> **Join hands and walk to the left, left, left!**
> **Stop! Smile and say, "Please, please, please!**
>
> **Walk to the center of the circle, circle, circle,**
> **then back to your place, place, place!**
> **Put your hands to your ears, ears, ears,**
> **and make a funny, silly, face, face, face!**

Have the students return to a listening position and finish the lesson.

CONCLUSION:

Conclude the lesson by saying:

Boys and girls, I hope you will remember the rule that goes with *Paw #3*. Who would like to tell us what the *Paw #3 rule* is? (The rule is: Work comes before play. During work time, you should work. During play time, you may play. But don't play during work time!)

Give each student a copy of *Paw #3*. Then say:

> **Here is a worksheet with *Paw #3*. After you decorate it, I would like you to put it and your *Work Before Play* worksheet into your *A School Of Champions!* folder.**

When the students have finished, collect the folders and any other materials that have been distributed to them. Then conclude the lesson by saying:

> **Next week, Champ and I will come back and teach the *Paw #4 rule*. You are almost finished with all the lessons about being a champion. After you learn one more rule, you'll be ready to become a part of *A School Of Champions!*** (Make sure Champ barks once to say *goodbye.*)

Work Before Play

Name _____

#1

#2

#3

#4

#5

#6

_____
(NAME)

1 Work First, Then Play!

LESSON 5 – KINDERGARTEN
Champions Know How To Work Together!

Goal:

The students will learn why it is important to be able to work in a group and how to be good group members. They will practice working together in small groups.

Materials Needed:

For the leader:
- ☐ Champ puppet/stuffed toy with sticky notes #1, #2, and #3 on its paws
- ☐ *A School Of Champions! Kindergarten* song (optional, page 20)
- ☐ Sticky note
- ☐ Marker

For each student:
- ☐ *A School Of Champions!* folder prepared in Lesson 1
- ☐ *Paw #4* (page 57)
- ☐ Crayons

For each student group:
- ☐ 1 sheet of paper (11" x 18" or larger) for each small group
- ☐ Crayons

Presentation Preparation:

Reproduce *Paw #4* for each student.
Write *#4* on the sticky note.

Lesson:

INTRODUCTION:

Introduce the lesson by saying:

Hello, boys and girls! Champ and I are back to teach you the rule that goes with *Paw #4.* (Place the final sticky note with #4 on Champ's paw.)

After today's lesson, you will know all of Champ's rules. Next week, I will give you Champ's special award. You will then become a part of *A School Of Champions!* at _____ School!

REVIEW:

Review what was taught in the previous lessons by saying:

Let's go over all the *Paw rules* we have talked about so far. I want to make sure you remember each rule.

What is the *Paw #1 rule?* (Point to Champ's paw. The rule is: Try hard and keep practicing every day—even when things are hard. Never give up!)

How are you doing with following this rule? Are you trying hard each day? (Allow a short time for students to share their success stories.)

What is the *Paw #2 rule?* (Point to Champ's paw. The rule is: Sit still and listen every day. Review as much information as the class needs—body still, eyes on speaker, mind on what the speaker is saying.)

How are you doing with following this rule? Are you listening every day? I will be watching to see how you listen during this lesson.

What is the *Paw #3 rule?* (Point to Champ's paw. The rule is: Work comes first, then play. Don't play during work time!)

How are you doing with following this rule? (Allow time for the students' answers.)

It sounds like you are on the way to becoming a part of *A School Of Champions!* Congratulations!

SONG:

Lead the students in singing *A School Of Champions!* Say:

Before I teach you the final rule, let's sing *A School Of Champion*s! (Sing as much of the song as desired. If the children like to sing, feel free to sing all the verses learned so far. Otherwise, sing the first and last verses learned.)

A School Of Champions!/Kindergarten
(Sung to *The Wheels on the Bus*)

We are the champions at our school,
At our school, at our school!
We are the champions at our school!
We know how to win!

We're at school to work and learn,
Work and learn, work and learn!
We're at school to work and learn!
We know how to win!

We can do things when we try,
When we try, when we try!
We can do things when we try!
We know how to win!

So we try hard and never give up,
Never give up, never give up!
We try hard and never give up!
We know how to win!

We sit still and listen each day,
Listen each day, listen each day!
We sit still and listen each day!
We know how to win!

Following directions helps us learn,
Helps us learn, helps us learn!
Following directions helps us learn!
We know how to win!

Work comes first and then we play,
Work then play, work then play!
Work comes first and then we play!
We know how to win!

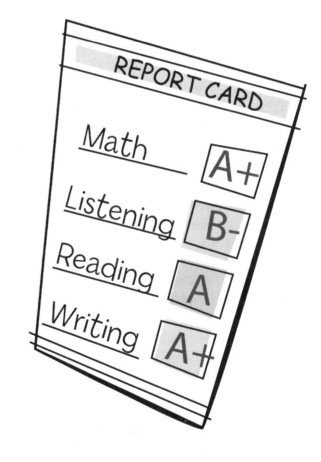

When you and the children have finished singing the song, compliment the students by saying:

Wow, you are great singers!

STORY:

Introduce the story by saying:

You have one more *Paw rule* to learn. Champ's class had to learn it, too. Let me tell you the story of how Champ's class learned the rule, without Mrs. Beagle even having to teach it!

One day, Mrs. Beagle told the puppies that she thought all of them had been doing a good job. They were trying very hard, listening, and finishing their work before playing.

Mrs. Beagle told the puppies that as a reward, they were going outside to play a game. She said that they would need a lot of room to play a chase game called *tag*. The puppies were excited about playing the game and hurried outside. But things out there were not very nice. The puppies looked around and saw that there were a lot of rocks in the field. Mrs. Beagle said all the rocks would have to be moved off the field before the puppies could play.

The puppies wanted to start playing tag, so they began picking up the rocks and moving them out of the way. Most of the rocks were small, and the puppies were able to move them easily. Using their mouths, they picked up the rocks and tossed them down the hill into a ditch that ran alongside the field.

There was one large rock that no one could budge. Jake, Champ's best friend, tried to move it by himself. But the rock didn't move one bit.

Then Trixie tried to move the rock. But Trixie was just a little puppy, and she couldn't move it at all.

Jake and Trixie asked Champ to move the rock. Champ thought he could do it because, as you can see, he's a very strong puppy. He pushed and shoved at the rock, but it didn't move.

Champ thought and thought. All of a sudden, he got an idea. He called all the puppies in his class together. "This is a big rock," he said, "so big that none of us can move it alone. But what if we all push together?" The puppies thought Champ had a good plan, so they agreed to try. When the puppies got behind the rock, Champ counted, "1, 2, 3!" They all pushed together and the rock rolled a little bit.

Champ said, "We moved it a little! Let's try again ... 1, 2, 3!" This time, the puppies pushed as hard as they could. The rock rolled out of its hole and down the hill into the ditch. The puppies were so happy, they let out a loud cheer.

Remember how the puppies in Champ's class cheered? (They barked three times.)

Let me hear how the puppies sounded.

When Mrs. Beagle saw what the puppies had done, she called everyone together. "I am so proud of all of you!" she said. "I didn't even have to teach you the last rule of becoming champion students! You are such smart puppies that you figured it out for yourself!"

The last rule is: When you work together, you will get more done and you will have fun doing it!

When the puppies heard what Mrs. Beagle said, they all cheered. How did they cheer? (Have the children bark three times.)

Then Champ's class began playing tag. Everyone had so much fun! And guess what? Champ tagged every puppy in the class!

DISCUSSION:

Ask the students:

What is the last rule that Champ's class learned? (When you work together, you will get more done and you will have fun doing it!)

That's our last *Paw!* Why do you think it's important to learn to work together in groups? (We live, play, and work in groups. Everything is more pleasant if you can get along with others.)

ACTIVITY 1:

Introduce the activity by saying:

Let's play a game to see how many groups you belong to. Please stand if you're a part of a group that I mention. (Give the students time to sit down each time after standing.)

How many of you are part of the group called:

a family?
a class?

a sports team?
a daycare group?
an after-school care group?
a musical group?

Wow! You belong to a lot of groups!

Groups are more fun if everyone gets along. What are some ways you can show each other that you want to be part of a group? (If the children can't come up with these answers, guide them and give them clues such as sharing, taking turns, being fair, using good manners, etc.)

Let's see if you can work together now.

Let's try clapping together. (Clap out a rhythm and let the students repeat the rhythm. Encourage the students to try to clap together so that it sounds like one pair of hands clapping.)

You did a great job!

ACTIVITY 2:

Introduce the activity by saying:

Let's try drawing pictures in small groups. I'm going to give each group one piece of paper and one box of crayons. I want to see if you can show me how members of a group can share, take turns, and be fair about the drawing activity.

Divide the class into groups of four or five students. Give each group one piece of paper and one box of crayons. Have each group draw pictures of familiar places, such as the zoo, a grocery store, a farm, a school, a back yard, etc. As the students are drawing, give loud compliments to the groups whose members are going out of their way to be polite, share, take turns, etc. Soon all groups will be trying to behave this way. When this happens, compliment all the groups.

SONG:

Lead the students in singing the next verse of *A School Of Champions!* Say:

Boys and girls, you've done a wonderful job of learning the rule for Champ's last paw: If you work together, you will get more work done and you will have fun doing it! Let's sing the verse about working in groups.

A School Of Champions!/Kindergarten
(Sung to *The Wheels on the Bus*)

We work and learn together in groups,
Together in groups, together in groups!
We work and learn together in groups!
We know how to win!

CONCLUSION:

Conclude the lesson by saying:

You have now learned all four of Champ's rules of being a champion. I'm going to give you a worksheet with today's rule on it. After you have finished coloring the page, you may put it into your *A School Of Champions!* folder.

Give each student his/her folder, a copy of *Paw #4*, and crayons. When the students have finished decorating the worksheet, have them place it in their folders. Collect the folders and any other materials that have been distributed to the students. Then say:

You and Champ are ready to become part of *A School Of Champions!* Next week, you'll each receive an award for all your hard work. I am excited that everyone in this class is a champion!

Champ, let's say goodbye for now. We'll be back next week. (Have Champ bark one time.)

Paw #4

_____
(NAME)

Working Together Is Important And Can Be Fun!

A School Of Champions! © 2007 Mar*co Products, Inc. 1.800.448.2197

LESSON 6 – KINDERGARTEN
A School Of Champions!

Goal:

This lesson is a review of all of the Kindergarten skills taught in *A School Of Champions!* The students will celebrate and be rewarded for their attention to the program.

Materials Needed:

For the leader:
- ☐ Champ puppet/stuffed toy with #1, #2, #3, and #4 sticky notes on its paws
- ☐ *A School Of Champions! Kindergarten* song (optional, page 20)
- ☐ Chalkboard and chalk or whiteboard and marker
- ☐ *Silly Monster* (page 63)
- ☐ Crayons or markers

For each student:
- ☐ *A School Of Champions*! folder prepared in Lesson 1
- ☐ 1 blank sheet of 8½" x 11" white paper
- ☐ *Certificate* (page 64)
- ☐ Crayons

Presentation Preparation:

Reproduce the *Certificate* for each student and fill it out. Make one copy of the *Silly Monster*. Color it if you wish.

Lesson:

INTRODUCTION:

Introduce the final lesson by saying:

> **Hello, boys and girls! Champ and I are back to invite you all to become part of *A School Of Champions!* at _____ School.**

In our other lessons, you learned some rules that will help you become champion students. I hope you've been proving to your teacher every day that you truly want to be champions.

Today is our last lesson, and each of you will receive an award for all your hard work and effort!

REVIEW:

Review what was taught in the previous lessons by saying:

Before we begin, I want to make sure you remember all Champ's rules.

Paw #1 **is...** (Have class say: "Try hard!" in unison.)
Paw #2 **is...** (Have class say: "Listen!" in unison.)
Paw #3 **is...** (Have class say: "Work then play!" in unison.)
Paw #4 **is...** (Have class say: "Work together!" in unison)

Great! You know all the rules. Now let's sing!

SONG:

Sing as much of the song as desired. If the children like to sing, feel free to sing all the verses learned so far. Otherwise, have the students sing as many of the verses as you and they want.

A School Of Champions!/Kindergarten
(Sung to *The Wheels on the Bus*)

**We are the champions at our school,
At our school, at our school!
We are the champions at our school!
We know how to win!**

**We're at school to work and learn,
Work and learn, work and learn!
We're at school to work and learn!
We know how to win!**

**We can do things when we try,
When we try, when we try!
We can do things when we try!
We know how to win!**

**So we try hard and never give up,
Never give up, never give up!**

We try hard and never give up!
We know how to win!

We sit still and listen each day,
Listen each day, listen each day!
We sit still and listen each day!
We know how to win!

Following directions helps us learn,
Helps us learn, helps us learn!
Following directions helps us learn!
We know how to win!

Work comes first and then we play,
Work then play, work then play!
Work comes first and then we play!
We know how to win!

We work and learn together in groups,
Together in groups, together in groups!
We work and learn together in groups!
We know how to win!

ACTIVITY:

Introduce the activity by saying:

Today, I am going to give each of you a special award to show that you have learned the rules of *A School Of Champions!* But before I do, you must show me that you really *have* learned all the rules.

We are going to do a special activity. You'll have to use many of the skills taught in *A School Of Champions!*

You will have to listen carefully. (If the students are sitting on the floor, have them return to their seats.)

Give each student his/her folder, a piece of white paper, and crayons. Then say:

Look at your crayons. Choose one to use during this activity. You may choose your favorite color, but don't use a light color that won't show up on white paper. (Wait for students to follow this direction. Make sure all students are quietly waiting for you to give the next direction.)

I have a picture of a silly monster. You are going to draw a monster like the monster in the picture I'm holding. But I'm not going to show you the picture.

You're going to listen as I tell you how to draw it! (Hold the picture against you so no one can see it.)

Before we begin, I want to make sure you know about some shapes you will need to draw. (If necessary, review various shapes with the students. Remind the students what each of the following shapes look like by drawing it on the chalkboard/whiteboard: a square, a circle, a triangle, a rectangle, a straight line, and a wiggly line.)

OK, you're now ready to draw. (Give the directions slowly and make sure that the students are listening carefully and all eyes are on you.)

My silly monster has a head that is a square. Make a square near the top of your paper. (On the board, draw the outline of a piece of paper. Draw a square in the correct location to show the students where to start their drawings. You will not model the rest of the drawing, but you want to make sure each student starts in the right spot so he/she will be able to fit the picture on the paper.)

As you give the following directions, make sure the students are quiet and listening to each step. Keep looking at your drawing so the students know you are carefully describing your picture. Say:

This silly monster has two antennae, so draw two short straight lines coming out of the top of his head.

On the end of each antenna, there is a little circle. Draw a little circle at the top of each straight line you have drawn.

This silly monster's eyes look like little rectangles lying on their sides.

In the middle of each rectangle, there is a small circle.

His nose is a very tiny triangle in the middle of his face.

He has a big smile on his face!

His neck is a tiny rectangle sitting on its end.

His body is a big square.

His arms are two wiggly lines that come down from each upper corner of the square body.

His legs are two wiggly lines that come from the bottom of his square body.

His feet look like rectangles. Draw a rectangle at the end of each wiggly leg.

He has three buttons going down the middle of his square body, one under the other. These buttons are shaped like small triangles.

OK, I'm ready to show you my picture. Let's see if your picture looks like mine. (Hold up the picture. Most students will see a resemblance and be delighted! Compliment the students. Look at each drawing and point out the similarities. Some will not look like the original silly monster, but praise each child's effort.)

DISCUSSION AND AWARDS PRESENTATION:

Holding Champ, say:

> **Wow! If you can follow directions like that, you are ready to become a part of *A School Of Champions!* Right, Champ?** (Have Champ bark once.)

> **We're now ready to give out the *Certificates.*** (Call each child's name and have him/her walk to the front of the room. Shake the child's hand as you award his/her *Certificate.*)

CONCLUSION:

After all the *Certificates* have been given out, congratulate the class. Then say:

> **I'm expecting to hear great things about this class this year. You're going to learn a lot, because you are all part of *A SCHOOL OF CHAMPIONS!* Right, Champ?** (Have Champ bark one time.)

> **Boys and girls, this is not the last time I'll visit your class this year, but it is the last time Champ will be coming with me. Champ is going back to being a full-time student at *The Blue Ribbon School For Dogs*.**

> *Optional:* **I'll bring Champ to each of you and you may give him a high-five, a regular handshake, or a hug.**

Have Champ bark once as a farewell to the class.

Have the children add their drawing and the *Certificate* they received to their folders. Tell the students to take the folder home and tell their parents all about their special award.

Optional: Sing as much of the *A School Of Champions!* song as desired.

Silly Monster

_____'s
SCHOOL NAME

School Of Champions!

_____
NAME OF STUDENT

has completed the
Kindergarten program
for
A School Of Champions!

_____
SIGNATURE

_____
DATE

A School Of Champions!

Grade 1

TEST PAPER

A

A School Of Champions!
Grade 1
(Sung to If You're Happy and You Know It)

We're from a school of champions, yes we are!
We're from a school of champions, yes we are!
We're so proud of what we do,
And we work till we are through.
We're from a school of champions, yes we are!

We try very hard every day!
We try very hard every day!
We're so proud of what we do,
And we work till we are through.
We try very hard every day!

We listen to our teacher, yes we do!
We listen to our teacher, yes we do!
We're so proud of what we do,
And we work till we are through.
We listen to our teacher, yes we do!

We organize our desks and papers, too!
We organize our desks and papers, too!
We're so proud of what we do,
And we work till we are through.
We organize our desks and papers, too!

We use our time wisely every day!
We use our time wisely every day!
We're so proud of what we do,
And we work till we are through.
We use our time wisely every day!

We check all our papers for mistakes!
We check all our papers for mistakes!
We're so proud of what we do,
And we work till we are through.
We check all our papers for mistakes!

We study and prepare for all our tests!
We study and prepare for all our tests!
We're so proud of what we do,
And we work till we are through.
We study and prepare for all our tests!

How It Feels To Be A Champion!

Goal:

This lesson is an introduction to *A School Of Champions!* for Grade 1 students. The students will learn that they now have the important job of being a student. This lesson will motivate them to want to learn more about becoming champion students and help them realize that doing their best will make them feel proud and happy.

Materials Needed:

For the leader:
☐ Dog puppet or 4-legged stuffed toy named *Clover*
☐ *A School Of Champions! Grade 1* song (optional, page 66)
☐ Bag
☐ Chalkboard and chalk or whiteboard and marker

For each student:
☐ *Clover* (page 72)
☐ 1 piece of 11" x 18" construction paper
☐ Crayons

Presentation Preparation:

Place the puppet/toy in the bag. Reproduce the *Clover* worksheet for each student. Gather any other necessary materials.

Note: When presenting this lesson and the rest of Grade 1 *A School Of Champions!* lessons, it is recommended that the facilitator sit in a low chair facing students, who are sitting on the floor around the chair.

Lesson:

INTRODUCTION 1: (You may use this introduction if this is your first lesson of the school year in this classroom. If you've been in this classroom before, skip to Introduction 2, page 68.)

Introduce the lesson by saying:

Hello, boys and girls! My name is _____. Let me hear you say my name together. (After the students say your name, continue the lesson.)

Good! I want you to remember my name, because I will visit your classroom a lot this year. Like many other adults, I have a job at this school. My job is to help children learn and do well in school.

I want to see if you know about some of the other jobs people have at our school.

Do you know what the principal's job is? (To run the school or be the boss)

A person called *a secretary* works in the office. What is the secretary's job? (To answer phones, write letters, help the principal)

What about the school nurse? (To help kids when they are sick or get hurt at school)

What is your teacher's job? (To teach us all the things we will learn in Grade 1)

If you wish to call attention to other jobs in the school, continue asking questions. Then explain your job by saying:

I am the school counselor. I visit all the classrooms and teach lessons that help children do well in school and in other parts of their lives. In my lessons, I will be talking about feelings, friends, how to behave, and how to succeed in school.

Sometimes I'll come into your classroom, and sometimes I might invite children to come to my room to talk. You'll see me many times this year, and I hope I'll get to know each of you very well.

Did you know that YOU have a job at this school, too? Who can tell me the name of the job each of you has at this school? (Children who go to school are called *students*. Sometimes they are called *pupils*.)

Yes, it's true! We all have jobs at _____ School. And every job, including yours, is very special!

 INTRODUCTION 2: (If this is not your first lesson of the year in this classroom, use this introduction.)

Hello, boys and girls! Who remembers my name? (Have the students raise their hands if they remember your name.)

Who remembers what my job is at this school? (School counselor or whatever the title of your job is)

What is (<u>USE THE TEACHER'S NAME</u>) job at this school? (To teach us all the things we will learn in Grade 1)

Great! And what is your job at this school? (Student)

Yes, it's true! We all have jobs at _____ School. And each job, including yours, is very special!

DISCUSSION: Whether you used Introduction 1 or 2, continue the lesson by saying:

Congratulations on having an important job! Being a Grade 1 student at ____ _____ School is important. Just like the principal or the nurse or your teacher or the secretary or the counselor, we all have special things to do at this school.

As a Grade 1 student, what do you think you will be doing each day at school? (Lead the students to an appropriate answer. A Grade 1 student's job is to work and learn Grade 1 lessons such as learning to read, write, and do math.)

Whenever you have a job, it's important to do your best. I try every day to be the best counselor I can be. Do all of you feel the same way about being the best student you can be? (Hopefully, everyone will nod or say, "Yes!")

That's great! When you're doing your best job, you're proving that you are a champion!

What do you think it means to be a champion? (A champion is a winner and a champion student is a student who tries to do his or her best in school every day.)

Wouldn't it be wonderful if we had a whole school of champions? (Hopefully, all the students will agree.)

Champions feel good about what they are doing … whether anyone is around to watch them or not. In fact, when I'm doing my best job, you can tell by looking at me. My face and body look like this. (Model upright posture and a proud, smiling face.)

Let me see each of you look like that. (Allow time for the children to assume the position.)

What feeling words would describe the way we all look right now? (Happy, proud, satisfied, etc.)

A School Of Champions! © 2007 Mar*co Products, Inc. 1.800.448.2197

You already know what a champion looks like. In the next few weeks, I'm going to visit your classroom to give you some tips on how to do your best in school. In fact, I'll teach you how to be champion students!

I would like to introduce you to a friend of mine who also wants to be a champion student. This is Clover! (Take Clover out of the bag and have him bark one time for the students.)

Clover is a first-grade student, just like you. (*Note:* If this program was presented to the students in Kindergarten, explain that Clover is Champ's litter mate or brother, who they were introduced to last year.) **The name of his school is *The Blue Ribbon School For Dogs,* and his teacher is Mrs. Hound. Clover wants to be a champion, just like you. So I'll bring him with me when I teach you how to be champion students!**

OK, Clover? (Have Clover bark once.)

SONG:

Introduce the song by saying:

I know a song about being champion students. I'd like to teach you this song so we can sing it together. After I sing the words, I'd like you to sing the song with me.

A School Of Champions!/Grade 1
(Sung to *If You're Happy and You Know It*)

We're from a school of champions, yes we are!
We're from a school of champions, yes we are!
We're so proud of what we do,
And we work till we are through.
We're from a school of champions, yes we are!

When you and the children have finished singing the song, compliment the students by saying:

Great job!

ACTIVITY:

Send the students to their seats. Then say:

I have a picture of Clover for you to keep. Today, we're going to make a folder to hold this picture and all the papers you'll be getting from me in the next few weeks.

Give each student a copy of *Clover*, construction paper, and crayons. Then say:

To make your folder, fold your construction paper in half. (Demonstrate folding the paper.)

Write *A School Of Champions!* on the board for the students. Point to each word and read it for the class. Then say:

Now I want you to write *A School Of Champions!* in very big letters at the top of your paper. Print your name at the bottom of the page. I will come around and help you if you need help doing this. You may decorate your folder any way you like. While you're waiting for me to help you write, you may color the picture of Clover.

CONCLUSION:

Tell the students to put the colored picture of Clover into their folders. Collect the folders. Then say:

Boys and girls, Clover and I are going to leave now. But we'll be back to teach you how to be champion students. We will have *A School Of Champions!* Let's sing our song one more time.

Sing the first verse of *A School Of Champions!* with the students.

A School Of Champions!/Grade 1
(Sung to *If You're Happy and You Know It*)

We're from a school of champions, yes we are!
We're from a school of champions, yes we are!
We're so proud of what we do,
And we work till we are through.
We're from a school of champions, yes we are!

Clover

_____

(NAME)

Champions Try Hard Each Day!

Goal:

The students will learn that trying hard and not giving up even when tasks are difficult is the first important rule of becoming a champion student.

Materials Needed:

For the leader:
- ☐ Dog puppet or 4-legged stuffed toy named *Clover*
- ☐ *A School Of Champions! Grade 1* song (optional, page 66)
- ☐ Bag

For each student:
- ☐ *A School Of Champions!* folder
- ☐ *Try Very Hard Every Day And Never Give Up!* (page 79)
- ☐ Crayons

Presentation Preparation:

Place the puppet/toy in the bag. Reproduce *Try Very Hard Every Day And Never Give Up!* for each student. Gather any other necessary materials.

Lesson:

INTRODUCTION:

Take Clover out of the bag and wait for the students to give you their attention. Then say:

Last week, you told me that you all wanted to be champion students.

We learned a song about being part of *A School Of Champions*! Let's sing it together:

(Sung to *If You're Happy and You Know It*)

We're from a school of champions, yes we are!
We're from a school of champions, yes we are!
We're so proud of what we do,
And we work till we are through.
We're from a school of champions, yes we are!

Continue the lesson by saying:

Clover wants to be a champion student at his school, *The Blue Ribbon School For Dogs*. Don't you, Clover? (Have Clover bark once.)

But Clover knows that being a champion isn't always easy. He has had a few problems performing like a champion in school. So he wants to listen to these lessons, too. (Have Clover nod his head.)

Today, you're going to learn the first lesson about becoming a champion student. Let me start by telling you a little story about Clover. (Have Clover look up at the children and bark once.)

STORY:

Introduce the story by saying:

Here's what happened to Clover in school last week. His teacher, Mrs. Hound, told the students she was going to teach them a new trick. Everyone was excited, including Clover.

Mrs. Hound told the students she would show them the trick, then ask each student to try to do it.

Mrs. Hound took a tennis ball into her mouth, tossed it high into the air, then caught it in her mouth. She looked at the class and said, "OK, puppies! Do you think you can do that?" All the puppies in the class were anxious to try. Including Clover.

Clover was so excited that he couldn't wait another minute to try. He pushed his nose and mouth up, but the ball didn't even leave his mouth! Clover was upset. He tried again. The ball dribbled out of his mouth and landed on the floor, right beside his paws.

"What's wrong with me?" Clover thought to himself.

He looked around and saw many of his friends doing the trick perfectly. But Clover also noticed a few puppies, like him, who were having trouble.

Clover decided to try again. But when he tried flipping the ball up into the air, it fell out of his mouth, landed on the ground, and rolled away.

Clover was very disappointed in himself. He was sure there must be something wrong with him. He left the tennis ball where it was and went to the corner to cry.

Randy, one of Clover's closest friends, saw what happened. Randy told Mrs. Hound that Clover was crying in the corner of the room.

Mrs. Hound went to Clover and asked, "What's wrong?"

Clover couldn't even look at his teacher. He said in a low voice, "I CAN'T do it."

Mrs. Hound said, "Sure you can, Clover! Try again."

Clover said, "I can't DO it! I will NEVER be able to do it."

Mrs. Hound called all the puppies together. She asked how many were having difficulty doing the trick. Several of the puppies looked embarrassed, but held up their paws. Mrs. Hound told Clover and the rest of the puppies that champions must realize that not everything is easy at first. She told Clover that when she was a puppy, she had to practice this trick for more than a week before she learned to do it.

Clover said, "But some of the puppies are doing it without practicing for a week. I'll never be able to do it."

Mrs. Hound told Clover that everyone is different. That trick might be easy for some, but those puppies might have trouble doing another trick. Mrs. Hound then told Clover something very important.

Stop the story and say to the class:

What Mrs. Hound said is very important. I want to make sure you hear this ... because it's the first step to becoming a champion student!

Here is what Mrs. Hound told Clover. She said, "Clover, if you say you will NOT be able to do this trick ... you won't learn to do it ... because you will have given up."

A School Of Champions! © 2007 Mar*co Products, Inc. 1.800.448.2197

Then Mrs. Hound said, "If you try and keep trying, I promise that you WILL learn how to do it!"

Mrs. Hound said, "You have to picture yourself being a winner. Then you have to keep trying and practicing until you become a winner!"

"Now, make a picture in your mind of you doing this trick. Imagine the ball going up into the air. Now imagine catching it in your mouth."

Clover followed Mrs. Hound's instructions. Soon he had a picture in his mind of himself throwing the ball into the air and catching it in his mouth. He felt proud. Mrs. Hound could see that Clover's attitude was changing. She said, "OK, now do it!"

Clover tried and he tried some more. He didn't do the trick the first time, or the second time, or the third time, or even the fourth time. But he didn't give up, because he had the picture in his mind of himself doing it.

Clover kept on trying and trying. And guess what? Clover was able to do the trick the 16th time he tried! YEAH, CLOVER!

DISCUSSION:

Ask the students:

Boys and girls, are there things you can do now that you had trouble learning to do? (Let the class tell stories of things they had difficulty with—tying shoes, riding bikes, playing catch, etc.)

Do you think everything you will be asked to do in Grade 1 will be easy? (No, there is going to be some hard work ahead.)

The first thing you must learn about becoming a champion is that you must have a good attitude. You must have a picture in your mind of yourself learning to do Grade 1 work. Then you must keep trying and trying until you can do it. Just like Clover! YOU CAN'T GIVE UP, EVEN WHEN THINGS ARE DIFFICULT!

Will you agree to try very hard each day of Grade 1? (Give the students time to answer.) **Even if things are difficult?** (Hopefully, the students will agree to do this.)

Great! That is the first step to becoming a champion!

A School Of Champions! © 2007 Mar✳co Products, Inc. 1.800.448.2197

SONG:

Sing the song and have the students repeat the words until they have learned them. Say:

Let's sing some new words to our song.

A School Of Champions!/Grade 1
(Sung to *If You're Happy and You Know It*)

We try very hard every day!
We try very hard every day!
We're so proud of what we do,
And we work till we are through.
We try very hard every day!

ACTIVITY:

Introduce the activity by saying:

Because you want to become a part of *A School Of Champions!* I've asked you to promise that you'll keep trying even when things seem difficult.

I want you to remember this important rule, so I'm going to give you a picture of Clover doing his trick. The words on the page say: "Try very hard every day and never give up!"

Give each student his/her folder, a copy of *Try Very Hard Every Day And Never Give Up!*, and crayons. Tell the students to write their names on the paper and color the page. When they have finished coloring, they should put the page into their *A School Of Champions!* folder.

CONCLUSION:

As the students complete their pictures, ask each one to restate the promise. Make sure each student says something such as, "I won't give up" or "I will keep trying."

Collect the folders and any other materials that have been distributed to the students.

Conclude the lesson by saying:

Boys and girls, when Clover and I meet with you again, it will be to teach you the second important rule of becoming a champion. I will check with your teacher to make sure all of you are trying very hard and are not giving up, even when things are hard.

I'm excited that we're going to be part of *A School Of Champions!* How about you, Clover? Are you excited, too? (Have Clover bark twice.)

Lead the students in singing both verses of *A School Of Champions!*

A School Of Champions!/Grade 1
(Sung to *If You're Happy and You Know It*)

We're from a school of champions, yes we are!
We're from a school of champions, yes we are!
We're so proud of what we do,
And we work till we are through.
We're from a school of champions, yes we are!

We try very hard every day!
We try very hard every day!
We're so proud of what we do,
And we work till we are through.
We try very hard every day!

Try very hard every day
and
NEVER GIVE UP!

Champions Know How To Listen!

Goal:

The students will learn the importance of listening and will learn good listening habits. The students will then be given opportunities to practice listening and following directions.

Materials Needed:

For the leader:
- ☐ Dog puppet or 4-legged stuffed toy named *Clover*
- ☐ *A School Of Champions! Grade 1* song (optional, page 66)

For each student:
- ☐ *A School Of Champions!* folder
- ☐ Copy of *You Must Learn To Listen!* (page 88)
- ☐ Crayons

Presentation Preparation:

Reproduce *You Must Learn to Listen!* for each student. Gather any other necessary materials.

Lesson:

INTRODUCTION:

Review what was taught in the previous lessons by saying:

Boys and girls, Clover and I are back to teach you another lesson so you can become part of *A School Of Champions!* (Have Clover wave at the students.)

Who remembers the rule you and Clover learned last week? (You must try hard and not give up—even when the task seems difficult.)

How have you been doing this past week? Has everyone been trying very hard every day? (If the classroom teacher is in the room, ask for his/her opinion.)

SONG:

Lead the students in singing the first two verses of *A School Of Champions!* Say:

We learned part of the *A School Of Champions!* song during the last lesson. Let's sing it now.

A School Of Champions!/Grade 1
(Sung to *If You're Happy and You Know It*)

We're from a school of champions, yes we are!
We're from a school of champions, yes we are!
We're so proud of what we do,
And we work till we are through.
We're from a school of champions, yes we are!

We try very hard every day!
We try very hard every day!
We're so proud of what we do,
And we work till we are through.
We try very hard every day!

When you and the children have finished singing the song, compliment the students by saying:

You did a great job!

STORY:

When telling the story, stress the word *LISTEN* each time you say it. You may wish to have the students say the word out loud with you if they'd like to do so. Begin the story by saying:

Clover has been trying very hard at school. His teacher, Mrs. Hound, has complimented him several times for his effort. And Clover has noticed that when Mrs. Hound asks the class to do things that seem difficult, he does much better when he tries hard.

But even though Clover has been trying hard, he had some problems at school last week. Let me tell you what happened last Tuesday.

Clover was very excited, because Tuesday was his birthday. As soon as he arrived at school, he began telling his friends that he was going to have a wonderful day and that he had brought treats for everyone. Clover was so busy talking that he didn't realize Mrs. Hound had asked the puppies to sit down and take their reading books out of their desks. As all of the other puppies quieted down, Clover looked around and realized that he was the only one still standing and talking.

Mrs. Hound looked at him and said, "Clover, why aren't you in your seat?"

Clover said, "I'm sorry, Mrs. Hound. I didn't hear you tell us to sit."
Mrs. Hound said, "Well, you must learn to LISTEN!"

Clover looked embarrassed and said, "Yes, ma'am."

Clover promised himself that he wouldn't be caught talking again when he was supposed to be LISTENING. He perked up his ears and tried very hard to LISTEN during reading class. Mrs. Hound asked everyone to read a story from the reading book. Clover really liked the story, because it was about a cat that got stuck in a tree. Clover became very involved in the story and wanted to see how the cat finally got down.

Suddenly, he looked up and noticed that the whole class was lined up for gym class. Mrs. Hound asked, "Clover, why aren't you in line?"

"I didn't hear you tell us to line up," said Clover.

"Well, Clover," Mrs. Hound said, "you have to learn to _____!" (Have class say *listen*.)

"Yes, ma'am," said Clover as he quickly got in line.

Poor Clover! It was his birthday, and his teacher already had to scold him two times. But that isn't all that happened …

At lunch recess, Clover was able to forget his problems and really have a good time. The puppies were playing a fun game with a ball. One time, Clover had to run really fast and far to find the ball. When he finally found it, he looked up and realized that his class had already gone inside.

He ran as fast as he could into his classroom. Mrs. Hound looked and him and asked, "Clover, why are you late coming in from recess?"

Clover said, "I didn't hear the whistle!"

"Clover, you have to learn to _____!" Mrs. Hound said, again. (Again, let class say *listen* out loud.)

"Yes, ma'am," Clover said, again.

Poor Clover! It was his birthday, and he wasn't having such a great day. He started thinking that things would be better at home. He was sure his mom was baking a cake and would have presents for him. Clover loved cake, and he hoped his mom was baking his favorite kind. Clover continued thinking about the great time he'd have when he got home.

All of a sudden, Clover looked up and saw that all the puppies were gone. His teacher was just coming in from taking the class to the bus.

"Clover!" Mrs. Hound exclaimed. "Why are you still here? All of the rest of the puppies have gone home!"

This was just too much for Clover to bear. He started to cry! "I didn't hear you call for us to line up!"

"Clover," Mrs. Hound said, "you have to learn to _____!" (One more time, let the class say *listen* out loud.)

DISCUSSION:

Begin the discussion by saying:

The next day, Mrs. Hound asked the school nurse to check Clover's ears. But Clover's hearing was fine. The problem isn't that Clover can't HEAR. The problem is that he doesn't always _____! (Have the class say *listen* out loud.)

What is the difference between hearing and listening? (Hearing is done with only the ears. Listening takes more effort.)

Clap loudly one time. Then say:

Hearing has to do with ears only. How many of you heard that sound? (Allow time for a show of hands.)

Listening is more complicated. In the story, could Clover hear? (Yes, his teacher had the school nurse check his hearing.)

Why didn't Clover hear his teacher? (1. In the morning, he was talking while the teacher was talking. It's almost impossible to listen and talk at the same time. 2. Clover was reading. His mind was on the story. 3. Clover was having a good time chasing the ball and wasn't paying attention to anything else. 4. Clover's mind was on the cake his mom was going to bake.)

In those examples, it was not Clover's ears that didn't work. The problem was that his mind wasn't on what the teacher was saying.

So that you don't make the same mistake, here are the steps that will make you a good listener:

Your body must be still. (Moving around can be distracting. If you are playing with your fingers, you might be more focused on your fingers than on what the speaker is saying.)

Your eyes must be on the speaker. (Looking at the speaker helps you focus on what the speaker is saying.)

Your brain must be paying attention to what the speaker is saying.

Another important rule is that you shouldn't move until the speaker has finished talking. I have been in many classrooms and I've seen students make a big mistake when it comes to listening to directions. For example, I might say, "Today, we're going to be coloring a picture…" and kids start getting their crayons out right in the middle of what I am saying!

What's wrong with that? (Students who start moving around while the speaker is still speaking won't hear the end of the sentence.)

So another important rule is:

Listen carefully to everything the teacher is saying. Don't do anything but listen until the teacher has finished speaking.

ACTIVITY 1:

Tell the students:

Let's practice:

First of all, let me see if you're ready. Are your bodies still? (Look around the room and make eye contact with every student.)

Are your eyes on me? (Look at each student again.)

Are you thinking about what I'm saying? (Students will probably nod.)

OK, I'm going to give you some directions to follow. Let's see how well you can listen.

Stand up, turn around one time, and sit down. (If students begin to stand up while you're speaking, say, "STOP! Remember: You must listen to everything I say!")

Note: Each time you give a direction, stop any student from moving until you've finished giving the direction. Smile when you give this reminder, so no student's feelings will be hurt.

Stand up, stretch to the ceiling, touch your toes, and sit down.

Note: After the students follow each direction, praise their efforts and listening ability!

Stand up, raise one arm, put your arm down, and sit down.

Wave at me, pat your head, then pat your stomach. (Many students will begin to rise, because the previous directions began with standing. Stop the students from standing. Then explain that since they thought they knew what the direction would be, they didn't listen to what it was. Tell the students that this is a common mistake in school. Students think they know what's coming, so they don't always listen!

I will give you one more direction to follow. How many of you want to try a really hard one? (Most students will be having fun and want to try to follow a difficult direction.)

OK! Stand up, turn around once, pat your head, wave at me, and sit down.

This direction may confuse the students because it has five parts. Give the students the following information:

Boys and girls, some children say to me, "I'm trying to listen, but I can't remember all that stuff!" I want to teach you a trick that will help you. I want you to pretend you have a small tape recorder in your head.

What does a tape recorder do? (It repeats the words it has recorded. If I say, "Good morning!" the recorder will say, "Good morning!" if I push the *play* button.)

That's what I want you to do with my words. If I say, "Stand up and turn around one time," I want you to say those words in your head before you follow the direction.

Are you ready to try again to follow the difficult direction?

Stand up, turn around once, pat your head, wave at me, and sit down. (Make sure the students are silently repeating your words. Praise students who are mouthing the directions.)

Great job! You have just learned the second important rule of becoming a champion student: YOU MUST TO LEARN TO _____! (Give students the opportunity to say *listen*!)

A School Of Champions! © 2007 Mar★co Products, Inc. 1.800.448.2197

SONG:

Introduce the song by saying:

Let's sing some new words to our song. (Sing the song and have the students repeat the words until they have learned them.)

A School Of Champions!/Grade 1
(Sung to *If You're Happy and You Know It*)

We listen to our teacher, yes we do!
We listen to our teacher, yes we do!
We're so proud of what we do,
And we work till we are through.
We listen to our teacher, yes we do!

ACTIVITY 2:

Introduce the second activity by saying:

I want you to remember this second important rule, so I'm going to give you a picture of Clover listening to his teacher. The words on the page say: "You must learn to LISTEN!"

Give each student his/her folder, a copy of *You Must Learn To Listen!,* and crayons. Tell the students to write their names on their paper and that when they finish coloring the page, they may put it into their *A School Of Champions!* folder.

CONCLUSION:

Have the students put their papers into their folder. Collect the folders and any other materials that have been distributed to the students.

Conclude the lesson by saying:

Boys and girls, Clover and I will be back to teach you another important rule of becoming a champion student. I will check with your teacher to make sure each of you is trying to do your best every day and that you're using your ears, eyes, and mind to _____. (Have the students say *listen* out loud.)

I am excited that you're working to become a part of *A School Of Champions!*

Lead the students in singing *A School Of Champions!*

A School of Champions/Grade 1
(Sung to *If You're Happy and You Know It*)

We're from a school of champions, yes we are!
We're from a school of champions, yes we are!
We're so proud of what we do,
And we work till we are through.
We're from a school of champions, yes we are!

We try very hard every day!
We try very hard every day!
We're so proud of what we do,
And we work till we are through.
We try very hard every day!

We listen to our teacher, yes we do!
We listen to our teacher, yes we do!
We're so proud of what we do,
And we work till we are through.
We listen to our teacher, yes we do!

87

(NAME)

You Must Learn To
LISTEN!

Champions Are Organized!

Goal:

The students will learn what it means to be organized and then learn some organizational tips. The students will be given time to organize their desks and materials.

Materials Needed:

For the leader:
- ☐ Dog puppet or 4-legged stuffed toy named *Clover*
- ☐ *A School Of Champions! Grade 1* song (optional, page 66)
- ☐ *Clover's Homework Before He Got Organized* (page 95)
- ☐ *Clover's Homework After He Got Organized* (page 96)

For each student:
- ☐ *You Must Get Organized!* (page 97)
- ☐ Crayons
- ☐ *A School Of Champions!* folder

Presentation Preparation:

Reproduce *Clover's Homework Before He Got Organized* and *Clover's Homework After He Got Organized* for the leader. Reproduce *You Must Get Organized!* for each student. Gather any other necessary materials.

Lesson:

INTRODUCTION:

Review what was taught in the previous lessons by saying:

Boys and girls, Clover and I are back to teach you another lesson so you can become a part of *A School Of Champions!* (Have Clover wave at the students.)

Who remembers the rule that you and Clover learned last week? (You must learn to listen.)

Have you been trying to listen during the past week? (If the classroom teacher is in the room, ask for his/her opinion on this question, too.)

Tell me what a good listener must do. (The listener's body must be still, the listener's eyes should be on the speaker, and the listener's brain must be focused on what the speaker is saying.)

SONG:

Lead the students in singing three verses. Say:

Let's sing the part of *A School Of Champions!* that we have learned so far.

A School Of Champions!/Grade 1
(Sung to *If You're Happy and You Know It*)

We're from a school of champions, yes we are!
We're from a school of champions, yes we are!
We're so proud of what we do,
And we work till we are through.
We're from a school of champions, yes we are!

We try very hard every day!
We try very hard every day!
We're so proud of what we do,
And we work till we are through.
We try very hard every day!

We listen to our teacher, yes we do!
We listen to our teacher, yes we do!
We're so proud of what we do,
And we work till we are through.
We listen to our teacher, yes we do!

When you and the children have finished singing the song, compliment them by saying:

Great job! Now I'll tell you how Clover is doing in school.

STORY:

When telling the following story, stress the word *ORGANIZED* each time you say it. Let the students say it along with you if they want.

Clover really wants to be part of *A School Of Champions!* at his school. So he's been trying hard every day and is doing a much better job of listening. But I want to tell you what happened to Clover this past week.

It started when Mrs. Hound told the students to get their reading books out of their desks. Clover heard what Mrs. Hound said. He tried to follow her directions, but his desk was kind of a mess and he couldn't find his book. He pulled out some papers that were stuffed in his desk. He found an old math assignment, but he didn't find his reading book. He found half a dog biscuit, but not his reading book. Then he found that his glue bottle had come open and his crayons were covered with sticky glue.

Mrs. Hound noticed that Clover hadn't taken his reading book out of his desk. When she asked why he wasn't ready to read with the other puppies, Clover told her he couldn't find his reading book. Mrs. Hound said, "Clover, you must get ORGANIZED!"

Clover said, "Yes, ma'am," and kept looking for his reading book. He finally found it and was ready to read.

Later, during math time, Mrs. Hound asked the students to turn in the homework she had assigned the previous day. Clover was happy because he had done his homework. He looked in his book bag. His homework paper wasn't there. He looked in his math book. His assignment wasn't there. He checked his lunchbox. His assignment wasn't there! Mrs. Hound had been watching Clover, and she finally asked where his paper was. Clover looked sad and said he couldn't find it. Mrs. Hound said, "Clover, you must get ORGANIZED!"

Clover said, "Yes, ma'am."

Because Clover never found that assignment, he had to stay in at recess and do the homework all over again. When he finished and took his paper to his teacher, Mrs. Hound said, "Clover, this paper is a mess! You must get ORGANIZED!"

Clover burst into tears. He said, "I don't know what ORGANIZED means!"

Mrs. Hound felt bad that Clover was so confused. She asked him to stay after school and told him all about becoming organized. Clover is now doing much better. So he wants me to tell all of you about becoming ORGANIZED.

DISCUSSION:

Ask the students:

What do you think the word *organized* means? (Students usually guess that the word means *keeping your desk clean.*)

Then say:

Actually, the word *organized* **means a lot more than keeping your desk clean. It means** *having a system of how you keep your desk.* **It means** *putting things in the same place and keeping track of your things in the same way every single day.*

If you keep your desk organized, everything has a place and you put everything back in that place every single day. If you are organized, you will never have to clean out your desk again!

If your teacher tells you to take out your crayons, you will know exactly where they are. They will be in the crayon spot in your desk. Being organized takes a little extra time, but it's worth it!

Papers can mess up your desk more than just about anything. There is a tool that can really help with that. Where can you put papers that will help you organize your desk? (Folders)

Yes, folders are wonderful! In this classroom, has your teacher asked you to bring folders to school? What are they used for? (Lead the students in a discussion of what their teacher has asked of them. If the teacher is in the room, he/she might join in the discussion. Most teachers welcome the opportunity to review the folder procedure in the classroom. If the teacher has not asked the students to bring folders to class, lead a discussion of how folders could be used to set up an organized way of doing things—a homework folder, a take-home folder, a clean-paper folder, etc.)

We've talked about how to organize your desk and materials. But organization means more than putting things away. It is also a system of doing things.

In the story, Clover couldn't find his math assignment. Why? (Clover couldn't find his assignment because he never puts it in the same place. He doesn't have a system!)

What could Clover have done differently? (Clover could have had a homework folder. Whenever his teacher assigns a page, he could put it into that folder. As soon as he finishes his work at home, he could put the paper back into the folder and put the folder into his book bag.)

What organized system could Clover use so he would always know where his book bag is when it's time to leave for school in the morning? (He could keep his book bag in the same spot. Then he wouldn't have to look for it in the morning.)

Another good tip for being organized is: Put all the things you will need for school into your book bag before you go to bed at night.

Here is a plan of organization that works well for many students:

During the school day, put things to take home on the edge of your desk.

When it's time to go home, pack your book bag.

As soon as you get home, (before you forget) take out any notes or homework papers that your parent must read or sign. As soon as a paper is signed, put it back into the appropriate folder and put the folder into your book bag.

It's not always easy to be organized. Some people are naturally organized, and some people have to work hard at it. I'm one of those people who has to work hard to be organized. (Admit this if it's true. If it's not true, omit that sentence. Many students will admit their ability or inability to stay organized.)

I bet there are some really organized people in this room. Maybe they will share some of their secrets with those of us who have to work at being organized. (Let the students share their methods. It may turn out to be a great discussion of organizational skills, and the facilitator could learn some new tricks!)

Let's talk about one more thing that can be organized: how you write on your papers! In the story, Mrs. Hound told Clover that his paper was not organized. Let me show you what it looked like. (Hold up *Clover's Homework Before He Got Organized* with the name in the wrong spot and letters or words squeezed together and not inside the lines. Discuss the paper's illegibility.)

But Clover is doing much better now. Let me show you his latest paper. (Hold up *Clover's Homework After He Got Organized*. Discuss the use of margins, putting the name at the top, keeping spaces between words, etc.)

THIS is an organized paper! Yeah, Clover!

SONG:

Lead the students in singing the next verse of the song. Say:

Let's sing a new verse of our song!

A School Of Champions!/Grade 1
(Sung to *If You're Happy and You Know It*)

We organize our desks and papers, too!
We organize our desks and papers, too!
We're so proud of what we do,
And we work till we are through.
We organize our desks and papers, too!

A School Of Champions! © 2007 Mar∗co Products, Inc. 1.800.448.2197

ACTIVITY:

Begin the activity by saying:

> **Now I'm going to give you a chance to organize your desk. I don't want you to simply clean your desk out. I want you to ORGANIZE it! Everything will have a spot.** (If there is a right way to fit the books or materials in the desk, demonstrate for the class. Some students want to stack books in the desk, but show them that this makes it hard to get the bottom book out. If there is enough room in the desk, have the students stand the books up with spines out, as they are in a library.)

> **Raise your hand when you've finished organizing, and I'll come and check your desk. If your desk is organized, I'll give you a new picture of Clover to put into your *A School Of Champions!* folder. You may quietly color until the end of class.** (As you check the students' desks, keep repeating the word *organized*. Recognize each organized desk by saying, *"That* is an organized desk!")

Distribute the folder of each student who has an organized desk. Give each of those students crayons and a copy of *You Must Get Organized!* If time allows after the students have organized their desks, have each student tell you about the system he/she plans to use to keep papers and materials organized.

CONCLUSION:

Have the students put their papers into their folder. Collect the folders and any other materials that have been distributed to the students. Then say:

> **Boys and girls, keep working to become champion students! Clover and I will be back again to teach you another rule.** (Have Clover bark one time.)

Optional: Sing the first verse of *A School Of Champions!*

> ### *A School Of Champions!/Grade 1*
> (Sung to *If You're Happy and You Know It*)
>
> **We're from a school of champions, yes we are!**
> **We're from a school of champions, yes we are!**
> **We're so proud of what we do,**
> **And we work till we are through.**
> **We're from a school of champions, yes we are!**

A School Of Champions! © 2007 Mar*co Products, Inc. 1.800.448.2197

Clover's Homework
Before He Got Organized

My name is Clover.

I go To schol.

I like to play with my freinds.

I want to be a champion student.

Mrs. Hound is a goood teacher.

Clover

Clover's Homework
After He Got Organized

Clover

My name is Clover.
I go to school.

I like to play with
my friends.

I want to be a
champion student.

Mrs. Hound is a
good teacher.

_____
(NAME)

You Must
GET ORGANIZED!

Champions Use Time Wisely!

Goal:

The students will learn what it means to *use time wisely*. After a story and discussion about how to use time efficiently, the students will be given an opportunity to practice *using time wisely*.

Materials Needed:

For the leader:
- ☐ Dog puppet or 4-legged stuffed toy named *Clover*
- ☐ *A School Of Champions! Grade 1* song (optional, page 66)

For each student:
- ☐ *Check Clover's Work* (page 105)
- ☐ *You Must Use Time Wisely!* (page 106)
- ☐ Pencil
- ☐ Crayons
- ☐ *A School Of Champions*! folder

Presentation Preparation:

Reproduce *Check Clover's Work* and *You Must Use Time Wisely!* for each student. Gather any other necessary materials.

Lesson:

INTRODUCTION:

Review what was taught in the previous lessons by saying:

Boys and girls, Clover and I are back to teach you another lesson so you can become part of *A School Of Champions*! (Have Clover wave at the students.)

Who remembers the rules you and Clover have learned so far? (You must try hard every day, listen, and be organized.)

How many of you have been staying organized during the past week? (Take a few moments to let the students share organization stories. If the classroom teacher is in the room, ask for his/her opinion on this question.)

SONG:

Lead the students in singing *A School Of Champions!* Say:

> **Let's sing the part of *A School Of Champions!* that we've learned so far.**
>
> ***A School Of Champions!/Grade 1***
> (Sung to *If You're Happy and You Know It*)
>
> **We're from a school of champions, yes we are!**
> **We're from a school of champions, yes we are!**
> **We're so proud of what we do,**
> **And we work till we are through.**
> **We're from a school of champions, yes we are!**
>
> **We try very hard every day!**
> **We try very hard every day!**
> **We're so proud of what we do,**
> **And we work till we are through.**
> **We try very hard every day!**
>
> **We listen to our teacher, yes we do!**
> **We listen to our teacher, yes we do!**
> **We're so proud of what we do,**
> **And we work till we are through.**
> **We listen to our teacher, yes we do!**
>
> **We organize our desks and papers, too!**
> **We organize our desks and papers, too!**
> **We're so proud of what we do,**
> **And we work till we are through.**
> **We organize our desks and papers, too!**

When you and the children have finished singing the song, compliment them by saying:

> **Great job!**

STORY:

Introduce the story by saying:

> **Now I'll tell you how Clover is doing in school.** (Hold Clover in your lap while telling the story.)

Clover is doing well. He's trying hard, listening, and staying organized. If you'd seen him in school this past week, you would have been very proud. But Clover had a problem last Tuesday. Let me tell you what happened.

Right after reading class, Mrs. Hound told the students that before they went out for recess, she wanted each of them to complete a worksheet and draw a picture about the story the class had just read out loud.

Stop the story for a minute and ask the following question:

Which sounds like more fun to you: drawing a picture or doing a worksheet? (Let the students answer. If they say they would rather draw, say that Clover likes drawing better, so he decided to do that first. If the students say they would do the worksheet first, say that Clover didn't choose to do the worksheet first. Tell the students that Clover likes drawing better than doing worksheets.)

Continue the story:

Anyway, Clover started by drawing his picture. Clover loves to draw, and he concentrated on making a beautiful picture. The story the class had read was about a boy playing in a field with his dog. So Clover drew the boy and the dog. Then he drew a field with lots of flowers and birds in the air and a tree nearby and clouds in the sky and …

All of a sudden, Clover heard his teacher say, "All right, it's time for recess. Turn in your worksheet and your picture."

Clover had to tell his teacher that he hadn't even started the worksheet. Mrs. Hound looked at him and said, "Clover, you must use time wisely!"

Clover was upset. "Yes, ma'am," he said. He had to stay inside during recess to do his worksheet.

After lunch that day, Mrs. Hound gave the class a handwriting assignment. Clover sat down to begin working, but he was distracted by a fly that kept landing on his paper. He watched the fly for a few minutes. It was making loops around his desk, and Clover wondered if flies plan their flights or just fly around to whatever interests them. When the fly finally flew away, Clover started working on his handwriting assignment.

Suddenly, Clover felt very thirsty. He got up to get a drink. When he got back to his desk, he broke the point on his pencil. He got up to sharpen his pencil, then went back to his assignment.

Just then, Mrs. Hound announced that it was time to turn in the papers. Once again, Clover had to tell Mrs. Hound that he hadn't even started the assignment. She asked why he hadn't done his work. Clover's answer was that he hadn't had enough time. Mrs. Hound said, "Clover, you must learn to use time wisely!" Clover was sad and told himself that he was certainly not going to make this mistake again. He didn't like getting into trouble.

Right after the next recess, Mrs. Hound gave the class a math assignment. This time, Clover started right away. He began working quickly and was the first student in his class to finish. When he took his paper up to Mrs. Hound, he felt very proud to have finished so quickly. Mrs. Hound looked at Clover's paper. But instead of complimenting him, she said, "Clover, look at this paper! It's a MESS, and you missed several problems. There is still 20 minutes of math time left. You could have used that time to check your work! Clover, you must learn to _____!" (Let the students answer, "Use time wisely!")

Poor Clover! He tries hard, but he's still having problems at school. Mrs. Hound talked with him about how to use time wisely, and he thinks he has it all straight now. That's why Clover thought today's lesson should be about what it means to USE TIME WISELY.

DISCUSSION:

Ask the students:

What does the word *wise* mean? (It has to do with *being smart.)*

What does *using time wisely* mean? (It means *being smart with your time.)*

Let's talk about time. How much time do we spend at school? (Help the students count the hours spent at school.)

How many minutes are in each hour? (60 minutes)

Each minute has 60 seconds. Does a minute seem like a long time or a short time? (Each child will have his/her own opinion.)

Continue the lesson by saying:

Let's play a game. Put your head on your desk. I'm going to say, "Go!" When you think a minute has gone by, quietly raise your hand. (Most children will raise their hands after 10 seconds. Tell the students when the minute has actually elapsed.)

That seemed like a pretty long time, didn't it? It's funny how quickly minutes can pass when you're being timed or when you're doing something you like.

In the story, what mistake did Clover make when he had to choose between drawing the picture and doing the worksheet? (He took too much time drawing his picture. It might have been better to finish the worksheet first. Then he could have spent the rest of the time on the picture. Many people like to do difficult tasks first. Tell the students that this doesn't necessarily have to be how they do things, but *Work Before Play* certainly seems to be a good rule to follow.)

Some people choose to do easy things first, then spend the rest of the time on the difficult tasks. But they must give themselves enough time to finish each task. Because Clover likes to draw, he went into more detail on the picture than he needed to. His teacher just wanted to make sure the students knew what the story was about. Clover didn't have to draw each blade of grass!

Ask the students:

What mistake did Clover make when he was supposed to do his handwriting assignment? (He wasted time. He daydreamed about the fly, got a drink, and had to sharpen his pencil.)

What could he have done about being thirsty? (He should have waited to get a drink until he had completed his assignment.)

What about the pencil point? (He should have had two or three sharpened pencils in his desk.)

What about the fly? (He should have paid attention to his work, not to the fly.)

What mistake did Clover make during math class? (He worked too fast!)

Using time wisely **reminds me of the story of the Three Bears. Some kids work TOO SLO-O-WLY. Some kids work TOO FAST! You must learn to work JUST RIGHT!**

Clover needed to learn that he must use each minute wisely. When you finish your work, it's always wise to use some of your minutes to check it.

When you check your paper, what are you checking for? (Mistakes)

Why would you want to find mistakes? (If you find them, you can correct them.)

If your teacher finds your mistakes before you do, what will happen? (They will be counted wrong.)

SONG:

Lead the students in singing *A School Of Champions!* Say:

Let's sing some new words to our song!

A School Of Champions!/Grade 1
(Sung to *If You're Happy and You Know It*)

We use our time wisely every day!
We use our time wisely every day!
We're so proud of what we do,
And we work till we are through.
We use our time wisely every day!

We check all our papers for mistakes!
We check all our papers for mistakes!
We're so proud of what we do,
And we work till we are through.
We check all our papers for mistakes!

ACTIVITY:

Begin the activity by saying:

I'm going to give you an opportunity to use time wisely right now. We have about 10 minutes of class left. I have a picture of Clover for you to color and add to your *A School Of Champions!* folder. And I have a paper of Clover's that has some mistakes on it. I'd like to see if you can complete both sheets before the end of class. To do that, you're going to have to really use time wisely!

Give each student his/her folder, a copy of *Check Clover's Work* and *You Must Use Time Wisely!*, crayons, and a pencil. Then tell the students to begin. As the students are working, occasionally compliment them on how they are using their time wisely. Hopefully, most students will complete the worksheet before starting to color. If someone asks to get a drink, ask if that would be a good use of the time left to complete the tasks.

When the allotted time has elapsed, use the following answer key to review the students' answers to *Check Clover's Work*:

ANSWER KEY FOR *CHECK CLOVER'S WORK*

Clover made 11 errors.

Sentences:

Sentence 1: Clover needed a capital letter at the beginning of the sentence, a capital letter to start his name, and a period at the end of the sentence.

Sentence 2: Clover needed a capital *I* and a period at the end of the sentence. He spelled *dog* incorrectly.

Sentence 3: Clover needed a capital *I* and a period at the end of the sentence. He used the wrong form of the word *run*.

Math Problems:

Problem #1 Answer should be 7.
Problem #2 Answer should be 5.
Problem #3 Is correct.

CONCLUSION:

Have the students put their papers into their folder. Collect the folders and any other materials that have been distributed to the students. Then say:

You have done a great job of USING TIME WISELY! Clover and I are going to leave now. But we'll be back to teach you one more lesson about becoming part of *A School Of Champions!* Our next visit will be Clover's last visit your class.
(Have Clover bark one time.)

Check Clover's Work

Directions for students: This is one of the papers Clover completed before he learned to use time wisely and always check his work. Clover made 11 mistakes on this page. See if you can find all of them.

Clover

1. my name is clover
2. i am a dig
3. i like to ran

1. 3	2. 1	3. 2
+4	+4	+2
2	6	4

A School Of Champions! © 2007 Mar*co Products, Inc. 1.800.448.2197

106

Champions Have Good Test-Taking Skills!

Goal:

The students will learn why they take tests and will learn about different kinds of tests. They will learn that a good attitude will help them do better in testing situations and they will be given an opportunity to practice taking a test.

Materials Needed:

For the leader:
- ☐ Dog puppet or 4-legged stuffed toy named *Clover*
- ☐ *A School Of Champions! Grade 1* song (optional, page 66)

For each student:
- ☐ *A School Of Champions! Test* (pages 113-114)
- ☐ *Be Prepared For Tests!* (page 115)
- ☐ *Certificate* (page 116)
- ☐ Crayons
- ☐ Pencil
- ☐ *A School Of Champions!* folder

Presentation Preparation:

Reproduce *A School Of Champions! Test, Certificate,* and *Be Prepared For Tests!* for each student. Fill out a *Certificate* for each student. Gather any other necessary materials.

Lesson:

INTRODUCTION:

Review what was taught in the previous lessons by saying:

Boys and girls, this is the last day Clover will be a guest in your classroom. I'll be back to teach other lessons. But after today, Clover will be a full-time student

at *The Blue Ribbon School For Dogs.* He has learned a lot about becoming a champion student. I hope you've learned a lot, too. Let's review the rules you and Clover have learned. To make it more fun, let's review by singing.

SONG:

Lead the students in singing all the verses to *A School Of Champions!*

A School Of Champions!/Grade 1
(Sung to *If You're Happy and You Know It*)

We're from a school of champions, yes we are!
We're from a school of champions, yes we are!
We're so proud of what we do,
And we work till we are through.
We're from a school of champions, yes we are!

We try very hard every day!
We try very hard every day!
We're so proud of what we do,
And we work till we are through.
We try very hard every day!

We listen to our teacher, yes we do!
We listen to our teacher, yes we do!
We're so proud of what we do,
And we work till we are through.
We listen to our teacher, yes we do!

We organize our desks and papers, too!
We organize our desks and papers, too!
We're so proud of what we do,
And we work till we are through.
We organize our desks and papers, too!

We use our time wisely every day!
We use our time wisely every day!
We're so proud of what we do,
And we work till we are through.
We use our time wisely every day!

We check all our papers for mistakes!
We check all our papers for mistakes!
We're so proud of what we do,
And we work till we are through.
We check all our papers for mistakes!

When you and the children have finished singing the song, compliment them by saying:

Wow! That song has lots of verses now! If you follow the rules we just sang about, I guarantee that each of you will be a champion student, just like Clover. (Have Clover bark one time.)

STORY:

Today, I want to tell you one last story about Clover. He has been doing very well at *The Blue Ribbon School For Dogs*. He has been trying hard, listening, staying organized, using time wisely, and checking all his papers before he turns them in. His mom is proud of him. His teacher is proud of him. And last but not least, Clover is proud of himself. And that's one of the best feelings anyone can have. Right, Clover? (Have Clover bark one time.)

Today's story is about a problem Clover had last week. The problem has to do with taking tests. Last week, Mrs. Hound gave the class a list of words and asked the students to practice spelling the words on the list. The teacher told her class that she was going to give a test the next day to see how well they had studied and learned to spell the words.

Clover worked very hard to learn to spell those words. He practiced by himself and with his mother. When his mom said the words, he could spell them. But on the day of the test, Clover was very nervous. He was afraid he might forget how to spell the words. He was so nervous … he *did* forget how to spell the words!

The mistake Clover made was thinking, "I don't think I'll be able to remember how to spell all those words." Do you remember the lesson we learned about trying hard? Do you remember we learned that you must believe in yourself in order to do well at any task? We learned that if you make a picture in your head of doing well, you'll be more successful in whatever you try to do.

Clover missed almost every word on that spelling test. Mrs. Hound kept Clover in at recess and asked whether he had studied. Clover told her that he had studied hard, but that he was nervous because this was a TEST! Mrs. Hound was very nice and gave Clover some tips that would help him do better on tests. That is what Clover wants me to share with you today. Right, Clover? (Have Clover bark one time.)

DISCUSSION:

Continue the lesson by saying:

Let's talk for a few minutes about tests.

Why do teachers give tests? (A test helps the teacher see how much you know or what you have learned. Taking tests is part of the job of every student.)

In the story, Mrs. Hound wanted to see if the students in her class had studied the words she assigned. She made up the test herself. That kind of test is called a *teacher-made test*. You will take teacher-made tests this year and in every grade. You will do better on this kind of test when you review and practice whatever the teacher asks you to do. The test could be on spelling, like the test Clover took. Or it could be on math, or on any of the subjects you study in school.

Your teacher, your parents, and the principal might want to see how much you know about lots of subjects. So your teachers might give other kinds of tests that you really can't study for. You won't always know all the answers to the questions on these *standardized tests*. The people who make these tests might put in some easy questions. But they might put some really hard questions in the tests, too, just to see how much you know. A test with only easy questions wouldn't show how much you have learned and how much you could have learned. For example, maybe you know Grade 1 reading words, but you know some Grade 2 things about math. This second kind of test will find out just how much you know. (Be as detailed about standardized or norm-referenced tests as desired. Give the students as much of the following information as you wish.)

Some tests are *timed.* The people who wrote these tests want all students to have the same amount of time to complete them as the students who first took them. You might feel that you didn't have enough time to finish a test like this. But as long as you tried your best, it's OK.

Some tests are scored by a machine, not by a teacher. On those tests, a student must be very careful with his or her pencil. That's because the machine has learned to read pencil marks and might misinterpret stray marks.

Keeping the test paper clean and neat is important. Because if the paper is wrinkled, it might not go through the grading machine properly.

Some tests are given every year in every grade at school. All students are expected to take these tests.

Continue the discussion by saying:

Clover learned that having a good attitude about tests will help him be a champion student. Mrs. Hound told Clover that by taking deep breaths and picturing himself doing well on the test, he would do better. She also gave him the following tips:

Before the test:

get a good night's sleep.

eat a healthy breakfast.

have a good attitude. (Mrs. Hound suggested that Clover say to himself, "I can do this!")

study the assigned material. Practice by saying out loud the words or math problems that will be on the test or even by singing them. It's OK to repeat and practice things several times. Do whatever you have to do to learn the information.

During the test:

listen to the teacher or read the directions. Don't think you already know what you're supposed to do. You might be wrong!

if a test is timed, USE TIME WISELY! Don't work too quickly or too slowly.

if you're allowed to choose an answer from a list, read all the choices before you decide on an answer.

do your own work. The teacher wants to know what _you_ know, not what your neighbor knows!

I'm happy to say that Mrs. Hound gave Clover a chance to repeat his spelling test. Clover took a deep breath and pictured himself doing well. And guess what? He did very well on that test, and he felt proud!

SONG:

Lead the students in singing *A School Of Champions!* Say:

Let's sing some new words to our song!

A School Of Champions!/Grade 1
(Sung to *If You're Happy and You Know It*)

We study and prepare for all our tests!
We study and prepare for all our tests!
We're so proud of what we do,
And we work till we are through.
We study and prepare for all our tests!

ACTIVITY:

Begin the activity by saying:

OK, you're going to get your chance to show me how much you've learned about becoming a champion student. You're going to take a test! (If the students groan, remind them of the importance of having a good attitude and thinking good thoughts. Remind them that they've been hearing the rules of becoming a champion student for the past five lessons, so you know they can do this.)

Give each student a copy of *A School Of Champions! Test* and a pencil. Read all the questions and answer choices to the students. Give them time to mark the correct answers. After the "test," review the answers and let the students grade their own papers. (This test is really just another chance to review the rules.)

CONCLUSION:

Conclude the final lesson by saying:

You've done it! You're now part of *A School Of Champions!* at _____ School. I'm proud of all of you, and I hope you're proud of yourselves. I'm going to give you one last picture of Clover to put into your *A School Of Champions!* folder. Then you may take the folder home to share with your parents. Tell them all about Clover and what he has learned and what you have learned.

Give each student his/her folder, a copy of *Be Prepared For Tests!,* and crayons. Allow time for the students to color the picture. Then say:

I also have a *Certificate* for each of you. It says you are a part of *A School Of Champions!* Congratulations!

Hand out the *Certificates* and give the students the opportunity to cheer for each other. Collect any pencils and crayons that were distributed. Have the students put all their papers into their folder. Then say:

Since this is the last time we'll be together, you may take your folders home.

Optional: Sing any or all parts of *A School Of Champions!*

Then say:

Clover, say *goodbye* to the boys and girls! (Have Clover bark one time.)

Optional: Take Clover to each student so everyone can shake his paw.

A School Of Champions! Test

Directions: Put an ✗ in the box next to the best answer for each of the following questions.

1. Clover learned that he had to try hard every day. You should try hard every day, too. What shows a good attitude?

- ☐ Trying to do something two times before giving up.
- ☐ Saying, "This is too hard."
- ☐ Not doing what the teacher asks.
- ☐ Making a picture of yourself being able to do something and practicing until you can do it.

2. Clover learned to listen. How can you become a good listener?

- ☐ Keep your body still.
- ☐ Keep your eyes on the speaker.
- ☐ Think about what the speaker is saying.
- ☐ All of the above are parts of listening.

3. When you listen, you will remember more if you pretend you have:

- ☐ A CD player in your head.
- ☐ A tape recorder in your head.
- ☐ An imaginary friend.
- ☐ A cup on your ear.

4. When your desk is organized:

- ☐ Everything has a place so you always know where things are.
- ☐ You stuff papers between your books.
- ☐ You never know where your stuff is.
- ☐ You can't find your pencils.

5. If you have an organized system of doing things:

- ☐ You'll have to search for your homework.
- ☐ You do everything the same way every day.
- ☐ Some days you will use folders and some days you won't.
- ☐ You'll lose your papers.

6. *Using time wisely* means:
- ☐ You do your work very quickly.
- ☐ You do your work very slowly.
- ☐ You daydream during reading class.
- ☐ You use the time you have in a very smart way.

7. Clover learned that it's always smart to take a few minutes to:
- ☐ Look at a fly.
- ☐ Get a drink during class.
- ☐ Check his papers before turning them in.
- ☐ Think about what his mom is having for dinner.

8. If you check your papers and find mistakes:
- ☐ You'll get a low grade.
- ☐ You can fix the mistakes.
- ☐ Your teacher will count the mistakes wrong.
- ☐ You'll be sad.

9. Clover learned that he had to take a few deep breaths before his test because:
- ☐ He knew all the answers.
- ☐ He didn't study for the test.
- ☐ He was holding his breath.
- ☐ He was nervous about taking a test.

10. A champion student:
- ☐ Tries hard every day.
- ☐ Listens carefully.
- ☐ Tries to be organized.
- ☐ Uses time wisely.
- ☐ Checks papers before turning them in.
- ☐ All of the above.

BE PREPARED
For Tests!

REPORT CARD

Math	A+
Listening	A
Reading	A
Writing	A+

_____'s
SCHOOL NAME

School Of Champions!

_____
NAME OF STUDENT

has completed the
Grade 1 program
for
A School Of Champions!

_____
SIGNATURE

_____
DATE

TEST PAPER

A

116

A School Of Champions!

Grade 2

A School Of Champions!
Grade 2
(Sung to Old *MacDonald Had a Farm*)

We are a school of champions—champ, champ, champions!
We work to win and try each day—champ, champ, champions!
With a win-win here and a try-try there.
Here a win, there a try,
Everywhere a win-try.
We are a school of champions—champ, champ, champions!

We are a school of champions—champ, champ, champions!
We listen to our teacher every day—champ, champ, champions!
With a listen-listen here and a listen-listen there.
Here a listen, there a listen,
Everywhere a listen-listen.
We are a school of champions—champ, champ, champions!

We are a school of champions—champ, champ, champions!
And every day we organize—champ, champ, champions!
With a book bag here and a folder there.
Here a book bag, there a folder,
Everywhere a book bag, folder.
We are a school of champions—champ, champ, champions!

We are a school of champions—champ, champ, champions!
We check our work, then turn it in—champ, champ, champions!
With a check-check here and a check-check there.
Here a check, there a check,
Everywhere a check-check.
We are a school of champions—champ, champ, champions!

We are a school of champions—champ, champ, champions!
We read all directions on our work—champ, champ, champions!
With a read-read here, and a read-read there.
Here a read, there a read,
Everywhere a read-read.
We are a school of champions—champ, champ, champions!

We are a school of champions—champ, champ, champions!
We study and prepare before all tests—champ, champ, champions!
With a study-study here and a test-test there.
Here a study, there a test,
Everywhere a study-test.
We are a school of champions—champ, champ, champions!

Champions Try Hard Each Day!

Goal:

The students will learn that the effort they put forth in Grade 2 will pay off this year and in the future. Students will learn that they can set long-term and short-term goals that will determine their success and their feelings about themselves.

Materials Needed:

For the leader:
- ☐ Dog puppet or 4-legged stuffed toy named *Scout*
- ☐ Paper bag
- ☐ *A School Of Champions! Grade 2* song (optional, page 118)
- ☐ *Word List* (optional, page 128)
- ☐ Scissors (optional)
- ☐ Container (optional)
- ☐ Chalkboard and chalk

For each student:
- ☐ 1 piece of 11" x 18" construction paper
- ☐ *Champions Try Hard Each Day!* (page 126)
- ☐ *Championship Bingo* (optional, page 127)
- ☐ *Word List* (optional, page 128)
- ☐ Scissors (optional)
- ☐ Glue stick (optional)
- ☐ Paper chips, poker chips, popcorn, or other materials to cover numbers on *Bingo* board (optional)
- ☐ Prizes for winners of *Bingo* game (optional)
- ☐ Crayons
- ☐ Pencil

Presentation Preparation:

Place the puppet/toy in the bag. Reproduce *Champions Try Hard Each Day!* for each student. If you are presenting the optional activity, *Championship Bingo Game*, reproduce *Championship Bingo* for each student and reproduce *Word List* for each student and for yourself. Cut apart the words from the *Word List* and place them in a container. Gather the other necessary materials.

Lesson:

INTRODUCTION 1: (You may use this introduction if this is your first lesson of the school year in this classroom. If you have been in this classroom before, skip to Introduction 2, see below.)

Introduce the lesson by saying:

Hello, boys and girls! For students new to this school, my name is _____. I am the school counselor. Welcome to our school! As I look around, I see many of my old friends as well as some new faces. (Look around at each student, smile, and make eye contact.)

I'll be a frequent visitor to your classroom this year. I conduct lessons in all the classrooms, and my lessons are meant to help students in many ways. Actually, my job at this school is to help you do your job!

INTRODUCTION 2: (Use this introduction if this is not your first lesson of the year in this classroom.)

Hello, boys and girls! You know that my job is to help you be successful at school and at home. For the next few weeks, I'm going to teach you skills that will help you be successful at your job this year.

DISCUSSION: Whether you used Introduction 1 or 2, continue the lesson by asking:

What is your job? (During this school year, each child's job is to be a Grade 2 student. That includes learning Grade 2 material and doing what the teachers ask.)

I'd like to help each of you do well at your job, so I'll be coming into your classroom several times to teach you study skills that will help you become the best student you can be!

***Study skills* are *hints* and *rules* that will help everyone do well in school.**

Ask the following questions in the tone a football coach would use to address a team before a game.

How many of you want to do well this year at school? (Hopefully, the students will all raise their hands. Tell them you want to hear some enthusiasm! Have them say, "Yes!")

How many of you want Grade 2 to be the best year you have ever had at school? (Encourage another enthusiastic, "Yes!")

How many of you want to be champion students? (Encourage another enthusiastic, "Yes!")

Well, I'm here to help you become champions! We're going to have so many champions that _____ School is going to be *A School Of Champions!* Let's hear it for our *School Of Champions!* (If students are getting too noisy, ask for a silent cheer.)

Continue the discussion by asking:

By the way, what is a champion? (A champion is a winner! A champion is a person who tries hard and succeeds.)

Then say:

When I use the word *winner,* it sounds like only one person can fill that job. In a race, for example, there is usually just one winner. But the word *champion* describes a certain kind of attitude and a certain kind of performance. Everyone in this room can be a champion … if you want to become one.

Before we continue, let me introduce a friend of mine. (Take the Scout puppet/toy out of a bag.)

This is Scout. (Look at Scout. *Note:* If this program was presented to the students in Kindergarten and/or first grade, explain that Scout is Champ and Clover's litter mate or sister, who they were introduced to previously.)

Scout, say *hello* to the boys and girls. (Have Scout yap and bark a few times and romp around.)

Scout, that's enough! Remember that we're in a school. So please settle down. (Have Scout look at you, then settle down.)

Scout sometimes needs little reminders to behave herself. I brought her with me because she has just decided she wants to be a champion student, too. She didn't always feel this way. In the past, she really didn't care how she did in school. But she recently changed her mind. Let me tell you her story.

STORY:

Begin the story by saying:

Scout goes to school just like you do. She is in Grade 2 at *The Blue Ribbon School For Dogs*. (If students were exposed to *A School Of Champions!* in Kindergarten or Grade 1, remind them that Champ and Clover are also students at that school.)

I'm afraid Scout hasn't always been the best student. Her problem has been that she loves to play and she doesn't always know when to stop! Just like a few minutes ago.

In Kindergarten and Grade 1, Scout did more playing and less focusing on her job of being a student. So you can imagine what her report cards looked like. (Slowly shake Scout's head back and forth.)

But in the last couple of weeks, Scout has been trying hard to make some changes. And it's all because of her new Grade 2 teacher.

Scout's new teacher is Mr. Beagle. He is a great teacher who always encourages his students to do their best.

On the first day of Grade 2, Scout did what she had always done. Being the playful puppy she is, Scout scampered into the classroom and began chasing her friends around the room. When everyone else stopped running, Scout was still so excited that she ran in circles and started to chase her own tail!

"Puppies!" barked Mr. Beagle. "I need you to sit down!" Everyone listened except Scout, who was having so much fun she didn't want to stop.

But Mr. Beagle firmly repeated his command. "Sit!" Even Scout could tell that Mr. Beagle is a teacher who means what he says and says what he means.

So Scout settled down. Mr. Beagle began telling the puppies what he expected of them in Grade 2. He told the puppies that they were not babies any more. He told them that the younger puppies at *The Blue Ribbon School For Dogs* looked up to them and copied their behavior.

Those words made Scout think. Did she want the younger puppies to act like she did at school? She realized she wasn't being a very good role model.

On that first day, Mr. Beagle also told the Grade 2 students that the choices they make every day will affect them for the rest of their lives. What kind of dogs did they want to be? Did they want to grow up to be playful pooches or did they want to be respected champions?

Mr. Beagle explained that picturing themselves in the future is a special way for the puppies to set a goal. Scout's teacher said that setting goals helps people focus on what is important in their lives. He said that remembering that picture would help the puppies make the right choices in school each day.

Scout knew what the picture in her head would look like. She could see herself standing proud and tall and successful. She pictured herself winning ribbons in dog shows and helping people each day. Scout liked that picture of the dog she could become. But to become that dog, she knew she had to make some changes. Starting right now, in Grade 2.

I wish I could say that Scout's new picture of herself has made it easy for her to always choose the right thing to do. Unfortunately, Scout has some old bad habits, and she sometimes forgets to picture her goal of being a champion.

Some days, it still seems easier and more fun to play, not work. But because Mr. Beagle is a great teacher, he is always there to remind Scout to keep the picture of what she wants to be fresh and in focus.

Scout is working harder than she ever has. She's trying to make each day of Grade 2 a wonderful learning experience. And that's what Scout wants for each of you. Grade 2 is your year to blossom, bloom, and become a champion ... just like Scout!

DISCUSSION:

Continue the lesson by saying:

If I asked you to make a picture in your head of what you'll be like when you're an adult, what would you see? I'm not asking you to picture what you'll look like, but how you'll feel about yourself. (Allow a few minutes for the students to respond. Guide the students to understand that no matter what profession they may someday choose, every one of them can be a champion—one who feels proud and respected.)

I look at you and I see champions. I'm looking at the future leaders of the world! Looking at you, I see doctors and nurses and teachers and scientists and inventors and athletes, anything you dream you want to be! I can picture each of you standing proud and tall and feeling good about yourself.

I'd like someone to come up and demonstrate how it looks on the outside when you're doing your best at whatever you're doing. (Choose a student to come to the front of the classroom. Have the student stand straight and smile proudly.)

This is what a champion looks like on the outside. What do you think a person who looks like that is thinking? (I do my best, I am smart, I try hard, and I am a champion!)

Let me see each of you stand up and look like a champion. (Have the students stand tall and smile.)

Wonderful! Please sit down.

As Scout's teacher said, when you have a picture like that in your head, you are setting a goal. You are picturing yourself as a grown-up. This is called a *long-term goal* because it is a goal you'll reach a long time from now. But in order to reach that long-term goal, there are things you must do now.

You must take advantage of your education today! You have a great teacher this year, just like Scout does, and everything you learn will help you become a champion in the future.

So the first study skill I want you to learn is: Try hard every day. If you make good choices and learn as much as you can every single day, you will learn a lot in Grade 2 … and you will be part of *A School Of Champions*!

Scout and I will be coming back to your classroom five more times, and we'll be teaching you other study skills that will help you do your best in school. Let's make Grade 2 the best year you've ever had in school!

SONG:

Say:

I know a song about being a champion student. I bet you'll be able sing it with me after you hear a little of it.

Sing the first verse of *A School Of Champions!* Then have the students sing along with you.

***A School Of Champions!*/Grade 2**
(Sung to *Old MacDonald Had a Farm*)

We are a school of champions—champ, champ, champions!
We work to win and try each day—champ, champ, champions!
With a win-win here and a try-try there.
Here a win, there a try,
Everywhere a win-try.
We are a school of champions—champ, champ, champions!

ACTIVITY:

Introduce the activity by saying:

I'm going to be giving you some worksheets and coloring pages during our time together, so I'd like you to make *A School Of Champions!* folder.

Give each student a piece of 11" x 18" construction paper, a pencil, and crayons. Then say:

Fold your paper in half to make a folder. (Demonstrate folding an 11" x 18" piece of paper in half.)

Write *A School Of Champions!* on the board and have the students copy the words carefully at the top of their folder cover. Then have them write their name at the bottom of the front cover.

While the students are writing on their covers, give each student a copy of *Champions Try Hard Each Day!* Then say:

> **Here's a picture of Scout. She has won a blue ribbon. She's thinking about something. Inside the bubble, write what you think Scout's thoughts would be about winning the blue ribbon. Then color the page. When you've finished, put the page into your new folder.**

> **Instruct the students to keep their folders in their desks until the next lesson.** (Or you may collect the folders after each lesson.)

OPTIONAL ACTIVITY:

Championship Bingo may be played now or before the next lesson as a reminder of words associated with being a champion.

If you have not already done so, cut apart the cards from the *Word List* and place the cards in a container. Give each student a copy of *Championship Bingo* and *Word List*, scissors, and a glue stick. Then say:

> **Let's play a game. Look at the list of words I gave you. The words have to do with being a champion. Let's read the words together. Raise your hand if you would like to volunteer to read a word from the list.** (Call on students who have raised their hands to read words from the list.)

> **Use your scissors to cut the words apart. Look at the sheet with blank boxes and the words *Championship Bingo* across the top. Choose the words you want to use. You won't need all the words. Glue one word into whichever box you'd like. When everyone has finished, we're going to play *Championship Bingo*!**

Give the students time to complete this task. Play *Championship Bingo* by drawing a word card from the container, reading the word aloud, then having the students cover or mark an X on the word if it is on their boards. If playing only one game, the students may use their crayons to mark off the words called. If playing more than one game, provide the students with paper chips, poker chips, popcorn, etc. to use as covers for words that have been called. You may want to obtain prizes for the winners.

CONCLUSION:

Conclude the first lesson by saying:

> **Boys and girls, Scout and I will be back (TIME/DAY YOU WILL BE BACK IN THE CLASSROOM) to teach you another lesson that will help you become part of *A School Of Champions!* at _____ School.**

> **This week, I want you to do your best each day. Remember your goal to be a champion in school and in the future!**

_____
(NAME)

Champions
Try Hard Each Day!

CHAMPIONSHIP BINGO

FREE SPACE

WORD LIST

🐾 CHAMPION	🐾 GOAL	🐾 EFFORT
🐾 PROUD	🐾 SCHOOL	🐾 TRY
🐾 WIN	🐾 DO YOUR BEST	🐾 LEARN
🐾 READING	🐾 MATH	🐾 WRITING
🐾 SCIENCE	🐾 BOOKS	🐾 BLUE RIBBON
🐾 FUTURE	🐾 SUCCESSFUL	🐾

Champions Know How To Listen!

Goal:

The students will learn that good listening is an important job of champion students. The students will learn how to improve their listening ability and then be given an opportunity to practice this crucial skill.

Materials Needed:

For the leader:
☐ Dog puppet or 4-legged stuffed toy named *Scout*
☐ *A School Of Champions! Grade 2* song (optional, page 118)

For each student:
☐ *A School Of Champions!* folder
☐ *Directions* (page 136)
☐ *Champions Listen Carefully!* (page 137)
☐ Crayons

Presentation Preparation:

Reproduce *Directions* and *Champions Listen Carefully!* for each student. Gather the other necessary materials.

Lesson:

INTRODUCTION:

Introduce the lesson by saying:

Hello, boys and girls! Scout and I are back to teach you another study skill that will help each of you become part of *A School Of Champions!*

Scout, say *hello* to the boys and girls! (Have Scout yap and bark a few times and romp around.)

Scout, that's enough! Remember that we're in a school. So please settle down.
(Have Scout look at you, then settle down.)

(Shake your head slowly.) **Scout is doing much better at making good choices in school, but she's such a playful puppy that she still needs a reminder to behave now and then!**

How are all of you doing? Are you trying hard, making good choices, and keeping in your mind the picture of the champion you want to become? (Allow time for the students to respond. If the classroom teacher is in the room, ask his/her opinion of how the students are doing.)

Last time I was here, we learned a song about becoming *A School Of Champions!* Let's sing it now.

A School Of Champions!/Grade 2
(Sung to *Old MacDonald Had a Farm*)

**We are a school of champions—champ, champ, champions!
We work to win and try each day—champ, champ, champions!
With a win-win here and a try-try there,
Here a win, there a try,
Everywhere a win-try.
We are a school of champions—champ, champ, champions!**

When you and the children have finished singing the song, compliment the students by saying:

Great job!

STORY:

Introduce the story by saying:

I want to tell you about how Scout has been doing this past week in her class at *The Blue Ribbon School For Dogs.*

As I just said, Scout has been trying harder than ever in school. For the most part, she's been making some very good choices about doing her daily work and behaving well, but she has some habits that are hard to break. Mr. Beagle, her teacher, is trying to be patient. But he's had to remind Scout to keep the goal of becoming a champion dog fresh in her mind.

One day last week, for example, Scout saw Toby on the way to school. Toby is Scout's best friend. Scout, being the playful puppy she is, shouted, "Bet you can't catch me!" Then she started to run as fast as she could run.

Toby accepted the challenge, and both dogs raced toward the school. Toby caught up with Scout and nipped her tail just as they were entering their classroom. Scout yelped, then tried to nip Toby's tail!

Mr. Beagle looked up from his desk as the two puppies ran into the classroom, yipping and yapping. "It's time to settle down," he said firmly. Both puppies stopped their chase game and quietly went to their seats.

See? I told you Scout is doing better! Scout only needed one reminder from Mr. Beagle before she went straight to her seat. Unfortunately, one reminder usually doesn't last for the whole school day.

After reading class, Mr. Beagle told the puppies they were going to play a game. Scout was excited, because she's an expert at playing games! Mr. Beagle told the class the name of the game was *Common Commands.*

Scout was happy to be playing a game at school. Mr. Beagle started the game by telling the puppies to stand. Scout stood with the rest of the puppies. Then Mr. Beagle said, "SIT!" and all the puppies, including Scout, quickly sat down. They followed the command at exactly the same time, so they grinned at each other delightedly. Scout liked this game!

Then Mr. Beagle asked the class to stand again. Scout was standing behind Toby. She noticed that Toby's tail was right in front of her. How tempting! She felt she HAD to give Toby's tail a quick little tug. Toby had it coming. Just then, Mr. Beagle said, "Sit up."

Because Scout was busy pulling Toby's tail, she didn't hear what Mr. Beagle had said to do. Everyone else in the class sat up at the same time. They all turned to stare at Scout, who was standing holding Toby's tail.

Scout was so embarrassed! She dropped Toby's tail just as Mr. Beagle said, "It seems that one member of our class is more interested in pulling tails than in playing the game."

Scout felt bad about her mistake. She thought she was never going to become a champion if she didn't know how to follow directions. Then Mr. Beagle said, "Roll over."

Once again, Scout was the only one in the class who didn't follow the command. She'd been so busy being embarrassed that she hadn't heard the new direction!

Scout was determined not to be embarrassed again. She decided to do her best to focus on what Mr. Beagle was saying. When she tried to keep her mind on what he was saying, she did much better at playing *Common Commands.*

By listening and focusing on what her teacher says, Scout has taken another big step toward becoming part of *A School Of Champions!* at *The Blue Ribbon School For Dogs.*

DISCUSSION:

Ask the students:

What was the point of the game Scout's class was playing? What did Scout's teacher want the class to do? (The purpose of the game was to have the puppies listen and follow directions. That's what Mr. Beagle wanted the puppies to do.)

Why is listening and following directions important to do in school? (Much of what students learn in school comes from listening to information teachers share.)

Why wasn't Scout able to follow all the directions when playing *Common Commands*? (Her attention was on Toby's tail, then on her own embarrassment.)

Then say:

In order for you to do a good job at listening and following directions, your body should be still, your eyes should be on the teacher, and your mind should be focused on what the teacher is saying.

ACTIVITY 1:

Introduce the activity by saying:

Let's play *Common Commands*. I'm going to give you some directions. Let's see if you can follow my directions.

Give the following directions clearly and slowly.

Stand up, then sit down. (Many students may start to rise as soon as they hear "Stand up.")

Have everyone sit down. Then say:

In order to follow directions, you must listen to everything I say. If you're busy getting up, you won't hear the end of the directions. Remember to listen to everything I say before you move!

Repeat the first direction:

Stand up, then sit down. (Praise the students for moving together and following the directions. Then continue the game by giving more complicated instructions.)

Stand up, turn around one time, sit down. (Stop students who move before you have finished giving the directions. Then praise the students for their listening skills.)

Stand up, raise your right hand, wave at me, sit down.

Raise your left hand and spread your fingers. (Some students will begin to stand, since all the other directions started with "Stand up." Stop the game.) **You have just made a very common mistake. You thought you knew what you were going to hear, so you didn't really listen to the directions.** (Repeat the previous directions, making sure students focus on you before you begin giving the directions.)

Continue the game:

Pat your head, rub your stomach, look at me, and smile!

Are you ready for a really hard one? (Hopefully, students will agree that they are.)

Stand up, touch your toes, turn around one time, and jump one time. (Many students will get mixed up because there are four things to remember. Stop the game and tell the students that you will teach them a trick for remembering long directions. Tell them to pretend they have a small tape recorder in their head. Tell the students to play back the directions as soon as they hear them. The directions will stay in their head for a few seconds. So repeating the directions to themselves will reinforce the words.)

Repeat the previous directions:

Stand up, touch your toes, turn around one time, and jump one time.

Compliment the students on the great job they have done.

SONG:

Say:

Let's learn another verse of *A School Of Champions!*

Review the words to the new verse, then lead the class in singing the second verse of *A School Of Champions*!

(Sung to *Old MacDonald Had a Farm*)

We are a school of champions—champ, champ, champions!
We listen to our teacher every day—champ, champ, champions!
With a listen-listen here and a listen-listen there,
Here a listen, there a listen.
Everywhere a listen-listen.
We are a school of champions—champ, champ, champions!

When you and the children have finished singing the song, compliment the students by saying:

Great job!

ACTIVITY 2:

Give each student a copy of *Directions*. Have the students take out their folder and crayons. Then say:

Let's do another practice activity, this time on paper. Remember that when you listen, your body must be still, your eyes should be on the speaker, and your mind should be on what the speaker is saying.

You will need four crayons—blue, red, green, and yellow. Repeat the directions in your head so you'll remember which colors to use.

Look at your *Directions* worksheet. I'll tell you what to draw in each paw print and which crayons you should use. Remember to listen to everything I say before you move!

When the students are ready, read the following directions clearly and slowly. You can make the directions easier or harder than those listed below, depending on the group doing this exercise. When the students have completed the *Directions* worksheet, have them check their own papers as you repeat the directions.

Paw #1   **Use your red crayon to make a circle inside the paw print. Put two blue dots in the middle of the circle.**

Paw #2   **Draw three straight blue lines and three wavy green lines inside the paw print.**

Paw #3   **Use your green crayon and write the letter that begins your first name inside the paw print. Draw a yellow box around this letter.**

Paw #4   **Use your blue crayon and draw a big X inside the paw print. Then put a yellow line through the middle of the X.**

Paw #5   Make a green square in the middle of the paw print. Draw a red circle in the middle of the green square.

Paw #6   Draw a blue smiley face with green hair inside the paw print.

Paw #7   Write the word *cat* in green letters inside the paw print. Underline the word in red.

Paw #8   Draw a red triangle inside the paw print. In the middle of the triangle, put three yellow dots.

Tell the students to put the completed worksheet into their folder.

CONCLUSION:

Conclude the lesson by saying:

Boys and girls, today you learned a second study skill that will help you become a champion. That skill is: LISTEN CAREFULLY.

You did a great job of listening and following directions during this lesson, so I know that you're on your way to becoming part of *A School Of Champions!* at _____ School!

I'm going give you a picture of Scout to color and put into your folder. Don't color during work time. That's not something a champion would do. Your teacher can decide the best time for you to color Scout's picture.

Give each student a copy of *Champions Listen Carefully!* Then say:

Scout and I will be back to teach you another lesson that will help you become a champion. Right, Scout? (Have Scout bark noisily and bounce around. Shake your head slowly and smile.)

Scout, remember that we're in school and that you want to be a champion! (Have Scout settle down a little more quickly than she did before.)

She's doing better!

Optional: Lead the students in singing *A School Of Champions!*

Directions

Name _____

#1

#2

#3

#4

#5

#6

#7

#8

A School Of Champions! © 2007 Mar✱co Products, Inc. 1.800.448.2197

Champions
Listen Carefully!

Champions Are Organized!

Goal:

The students will learn what it means to be organized. They will learn ways to keep their desk, papers, book bag, space, and time organized. They will be given time to organize their materials.

Materials Needed:

For the leader:
- ☐ Dog puppet or 4-legged stuffed toy named *Scout*
- ☐ *A School Of Champions! Grade 2* song (optional, page 118)

For each student:
- ☐ *A School Of Champions!* folder
- ☐ *Champions Are Organized!* (page 145)
- ☐ Crayons

Presentation Preparation:

Reproduce *Champions Are Organized!* for each student. Gather any other necessary materials.

Lesson:

INTRODUCTION:

Introduce the lesson by saying:

Hello, boys and girls! Scout and I are back to teach you another study skill that will help you become champion students.

Scout, say *hello* to the boys and girls! (Have Scout yap and bark a few times and romp around.)

Scout, that's enough! Remember that we're in a school. So please settle down. (Have Scout look at you, then settle down.)

(Shake your head slowly.) **Scout is doing much better in school. But because she's such a playful puppy, she still needs reminders.**

How are all of you doing? Are you trying hard and keeping in your mind the picture of the champion you want to become? (Give the students an opportunity to share. If the classroom teacher is in the room, ask his/her opinion of how the students are doing.)

And how are your listening skills coming along? Are you trying to keep your body still, your eyes on the speaker, and your mind on what the speaker is saying? (Give the students an opportunity to share. If the classroom teacher is in the room, ask his/her opinion of how the students are doing.)

SONG:

Sing *A School Of Champions!* Say:

Let's sing two verses of *A School Of Champions!*

A School Of Champions!/Grade 2
(Sung to *Old MacDonald Had a Farm*)

We are a school of champions—champ, champ, champions!
We work to win and try each day—champ, champ, champions!
With a win-win here and a try-try there.
Here a win, there a try,
Everywhere a win-try.
We are a school of champions—champ, champ, champions!

We are a school of champions—champ, champ, champions!
We listen to our teacher every day—champ, champ, champions!
With a listen-listen here and a listen-listen there.
Here a listen, there a listen,
Everywhere a listen-listen.
We are a school of champions—champ, champ, champions!

When you and the children have finished singing the song, compliment the students by saying:

Great job!

STORY:

Begin the story by saying:

I know you are all anxious to hear about how Scout is doing at *The Blue Ribbon School For Dogs*.

Scout is doing a great job listening and remembering her goal of being a champion. As I said, she still needs reminders from her teacher every once in a while, when she forgets to make good choices.

Last Tuesday, Scout walked quietly into her classroom and sat at her desk. Mr. Beagle told Scout she was being a good puppy. Then he asked her for the math paper that was to be signed by her mother and returned to school.

Scout knew her mother had signed that math paper. She looked in her desk, but she couldn't find the paper. There were lots of other papers in her desk … papers that were graded but not signed; papers that were not finished; papers that Scout hadn't started; and papers that were signed by her mom, given to Mr. Beagle, and given back to her. In other words, Scout's desk was stuffed with papers.

Scout knew her mother had signed that math paper. She looked in her take-home folder, but she couldn't find the paper. There were lots of other papers in that folder … papers that were graded but not signed; papers that were not finished; papers that Scout hadn't started; and papers that were signed by her mom, given to Mr. Beagle, and given back to her. In other words, Scout's folder was stuffed with papers!

While Scout was doing all this looking, Mr. Beagle was looking at Scout. He shook his head and said, "Never mind, Scout. You may give me that math paper when you find it. Just give me your reading homework that I assigned last night!"

Scout knew she had done the reading paper. So she looked …

I bet you know the story from here!

Mr. Beagle discovered that Scout has another problem in trying to become a champion. She has to get _____. (Ask if anyone knows the word. Let the class guess, *organized*.)

DISCUSSION:

Ask the students:

What does the word *organize* mean? (Many students think it means to clean out their desks or keep them clean.)

Then say:

To organize means *to have a system of doing things*. It begins with sorting through materials and putting like things together. But that is only the beginning! You must organize your desk, your papers, your time, and the way you do things.

Let's start at the beginning. How can you organize your desk? First, decide how you will sort the items in your desk and keep things in their places. When your desk is organized, there is a place for everything. If you keep everything where it is supposed to be, there will be no need to ever clean out your desk again! (The way the students choose to organize may have to do with the way the desks are built or the way the classroom teacher has requested the students keep their desk.)

Organizing your desk here at school is very helpful in becoming a champion. You can't do a good job if you can't find your papers and school supplies. It will help if you organize your things at home, too. I hope that each of you has a quiet place at home where you can do homework. Some of you might have a desk, and some of you might do your homework at the kitchen table. Wherever you work, it would be helpful to keep your supplies organized.

In the story I just told you, Scout had trouble knowing where her papers were. What could Scout use to help her become organized? (Scout could use folders in special ways. For example, Scout could use a red folder for notes to be signed by her mom. If she always puts notes to be signed by her mom into that red folder, she can get the paper out for her mom and put it back so she will know where the paper is the next day at school. Maybe she could use a blue folder for papers that are being sent home to stay and a green folder for unfinished homework assignments.)

Many students use folders, but don't bother to empty them when they should. The folders become stuffed with old papers. That's not being organized!

What do you think it means if I say you must develop an organized system of doing things? (Getting into the habit of doing something the same way every day.)

Students must get into the habit of doing the same thing every day. If you always put your homework sheets into a blue folder and put that folder into your book bag to go home, you'll always know where your homework paper is. You could take the folder out while you're working on the paper at home. Then put the paper back into the folder and put the folder back into the book bag so it will be where it belongs the next morning. When the teacher asks for your homework, where will it be? IN THE BLUE FOLDER IN YOUR BOOK BAG!

And where should your book bag be? (Wherever the student would like to keep it, but it should be in the same place every evening at home, so the student will not have to waste time looking for it before leaving for school.)

An organized person would also have a system of getting ready for school each day. When would be a good time to get notes signed and to prepare for the school day? (The evening before school is the best time to get things ready.)

You could lay out your clothes and everything you'll need for the next day. That is called *having a system!*

You could even organize your time! What do you think that means? (Organizing your time means making a schedule so you can get everything finished.)

Make sure you schedule time for homework and chores each day. Work then play is a great rule for champions to follow.

At school, many champion students work hard to complete all their work in the time the teacher has given them to do it. After the work is completed, champion students often read a book or do other activities suggested by their teacher.

Making a schedule for when you will complete your homework is helpful. You need to schedule time for homework every day, no matter what else you may be doing after school.

Some people are naturally organized and some of us have to work hard to stay organized. I am a person who has to work to stay organized. (Admit this if it is true.)

Let's hear from the people who are very organized. Will you share some secrets that might help the rest of us? (Give students a few moments to share. The facilitator will often hear tips that can help everyone in the class.)

ACTIVITY 1:

Begin the activity by saying:

Let's play a little game. I'm going to name some habits that students have. If you think it's an organized way to do things, put your thumbs up. If you think it is not an organized way of doing things, put your thumbs down. OK, ready?

Read the following list. Leave time for the students to put their thumbs up or down. Give feedback with each answer.

Some students shove graded papers into their desk. (Thumbs down! A take-home folder would be an organized place to put graded papers.)

Some students put their book bag in the same place each night. (Thumbs up! These students will always know where to find their book bag.)

Some students keep all their loose supplies in a pencil box. (Thumbs up! They can keep their desk organized and neat if all small things are put together in one place.)

Some students keep clean notebook paper in a folder so it won't get wrinkled. (Thumbs up! This sounds like a good way to know where to get a piece of paper.)

Some students keep every paper in their take-home folder and never unload it. (Thumbs down! Once the papers are graded and reviewed by your parents, you're supposed to leave them at home. Don't carry the same papers to and from school for the whole school year!)

Some students get notes and papers ready the night before school. (Thumbs up! It's not organized to run around getting everything you'll need for school five minutes before the bus comes.)

Some students have a system and do things the same way every day. (Thumbs up! That's what being organized is all about!)

Conclude the activity by saying:

Great job! I think you understand how to be organized!

SONG:

Say:

I have a new verse of *A School Of Champions!* for you to learn. Listen and join in whenever you feel you know the words.

A School Of Champions!/Grade 2
(Sung to *Old MacDonald Had a Farm*)

We are a school of champions—champ, champ, champions!
And every day we organize—champ, champ, champions!
With a book bag here and folder there.
Here a book bag, there a folder,
Everywhere a book bag, folder.
We are a school of champions—champ, champ, champions!

ACTIVITY 2:

Begin the second activity by saying:

In a few minutes, I'm going to give you a chance to organize your desk. (If students begin to organize their desks while you're still giving directions, stop and remind them they should listen to everything you say before they move.)

I have a new picture of Scout for you to color and add to your *A School Of Champions!* folder. I want you to organize your desk, then raise your hand. I'll check your desk, then give you the coloring worksheet. Remember: When you organize your desk, you're assigning everything a spot and you'll always keep it in that spot.

Let the students organize their desks. If the classroom teacher has a specific way he/she wants students to stack books or keep folders, have students share what they know about that system before they begin. The teacher may like to have an opportunity at this time to remind students of his/her expectations. As you check each desk, ask the student about his/her organized system of doing things. Give each student a copy of *Champions Are Organized!* and tell the students to put the completed worksheet into their folder.

CONCLUSION:

Conclude the lesson by saying:

Boys and girls, remember that today's study skill is TO GET ORGANIZED! This important rule will help each of you become part of *A School Of Champions!* at _____ School.

Scout and I will come back again to teach you another skill. Right, Scout? (Have Scout bark two times.)

I can tell Scout is becoming a champion, just like each of you!

Optional: Sing all or any verses of *A School Of Champions!*

(NAME)

Champions Are Organized!

145

Champions Always Proofread Their Work!

Goal:

The students will learn the meaning of the word *proofread* and learn that by performing this important task, they'll get better grades. The students will make a list of common types of errors to look for on their papers and will then have an opportunity to practice proofreading.

Materials Needed:

For the leader:
- ☐ Dog puppet or 4-legged stuffed toy named *Scout*
- ☐ *A School Of Champions! Grade 2* song (optional, page 118)
- ☐ A large piece of posterboard to leave in the classroom
- ☐ Marker

For each student:
- ☐ *Scout's Mistakes* (page 152)
- ☐ *Champions Proofread Their Papers!* (page 153)
- ☐ Crayons
- ☐ Pencil
- ☐ *A School Of Champions!* folder

Presentation Preparation:

Reproduce *Scout's Mistakes* and *Champions Proofread Their Papers!* for each student. Gather any other necessary materials.

Lesson:

INTRODUCTION:

Introduce the lesson by saying:

Hello, boys and girls! Scout and I are back to teach you another study skill that will help all of you become champion students.

Scout, say *hello* to the boys and girls! (Have Scout bark two or three times.)

Scout, that's enough! Remember that we're in a school. So please settle down. (Have Scout look at you, then settle down.)

(Shake your head slowly.) **Scout is doing much better in school. But because she's such a playful puppy, she still needs reminders.**

Then ask:

How are all of you doing? Are you keeping fresh in your mind your goal of the champion you want to become? (Allow time for the students to respond.)

Are you trying hard to be good listeners: using your ears, eyes, and mind? (Allow time for the students to respond.)

Are you trying to stay organized? (Allow time for the students to respond.)

SONG:

Sing *A School Of Champions!* Say:

Let's sing *A School Of Champions!* together.

Lead the students in singing *A School Of Champions!*

A School Of Champions!/Grade 2
(Sung to *Old MacDonald Had a Farm*)

We are a school of champions—champ, champ, champions!
We work to win and try each day—champ, champ, champions!
With a win-win here and a try-try there.
Here a win, there a try,
Everywhere a win-try.
We are a school of champions—champ, champ, champions!

We are a school of champions—champ, champ, champions!
We listen to our teacher every day—champ, champ, champions!
With a listen-listen here and a listen-listen there.
Here a listen, there a listen,
Everywhere a listen-listen.
We are a school of champions—champ, champ, champions!

We are a school of champions—champ, champ, champions!
And every day we organize—champ, champ, champions!
With a book bag here and folder there.
Here a book bag, there a folder,
Everywhere a book bag, folder.
We are a school of champions—champ, champ, champions!

Compliment the students on the great job they did singing the song.

STORY:

Continue the lesson by reading or telling the following story:

As I said before, Scout is trying hard to be a champion at *The Blue Ribbon School For Dogs*. Mr. Beagle has to occasionally remind her of her goal. But for the most part, she remembers the picture of the dog she would like to be in the future.

In spite of Scout's effort, she *did* have a problem this past week. Let me tell you what happened. Last Tuesday, Mr. Beagle asked for homework papers from the class. Scout had done the work and knew exactly where her paper was. It was in her blue homework folder, which was in her book bag, which she had packed the night before. She proudly handed her paper to her teacher.

Mr. Beagle took one look at her paper and asked, "Scout, haven't you forgotten something?"

"What?" asked Scout.

"How will I know whose paper this is when I grade it?" Mr. Beagle asked.

"Oh, I forgot to put my name on my paper!" said Scout. She took her paper, went back to her desk, and wrote her name at the top. Then she took the paper back to Mr. Beagle.

Mr. Beagle looked at the paper again and asked, "Now, what happened to Question #3 on this worksheet? Your answers go from #2 to #4!"

Scout looked at the paper. "Oh, I forgot to do #3! It will just take me a minute." She took her paper back to her desk, answered Question #3, then took the paper back to Mr. Beagle.

Mr. Beagle looked at the paper again and asked, "On Question #4, did you really want to spell *dog d-a-g*?"

Scout looked at the paper. "Oh, I made a mistake! I know that *dog* is spelled *d-o-g!* Let me fix that, please." She took her paper back to her desk, fixed the spelling mistake, then took the paper back to Mr. Beagle.

Mr. Beagle looked at the paper again and asked, "On the answer to Question #5, did you really mean to say dogs can *swam*?"

Scout looked at the paper and said, "Oh, I meant to say dogs can *swim*! Let me just take the paper back to my desk and … "

Mr. Beagle interrupted, "Scout, why don't you save both of us a little time and trouble? Take your paper back to your desk and check *everything*!"

Scout had just learned another important rule on how to become part of *A School Of Champions!*

DISCUSSION:

Ask the students:

What rule did Scout learn? (Scout learned that you must take some time to check your work before you turn it in.)

There is another word that adults sometimes use to describe the process of checking a paper. That word is *proofread*. You should always proofread your papers before you turn them in.

Why do you think it's important to proofread your papers before turning them in? (If you proofread your papers, YOU can find any mistakes you made before your teacher finds them! If you find the mistakes, you can change them so your teacher won't count them wrong.)

When you proofread your papers, what should you be looking for? (Any kind of error you might have made while doing your work. None of us is perfect, so we need to see if we can find any errors we might have made.)

What kinds of mistakes did Scout make on her homework paper? (She left her name off, skipped one of the questions, spelled *dog* incorrectly, wrote an answer that was obviously incorrect, and probably more!)

ACTIVITY 1:

Introduce the first activity by saying:

Let's make a list of the types of errors you should look for when proofreading your papers. I will leave this chart in your classroom so you can use it as a reminder every time you turn in a paper. Let's call our chart *Proofreading Checklist*.

Lead the students in brainstorming the types of mistakes they should look for on their papers. Write their answers on the piece of posterboard that will be left in the classroom. If the students repeat an item, compliment them, but remind them that their answer is already on the chart. If the students do not give the following suggestions, add them to the list.

- I have checked to see that my name is on the paper.
- I have checked to see that the proper heading is on the paper. (Ask the students what heading their teacher has requested. It might include the date, name of the subject, etc.)
- I have answered every assigned question.
- I checked my paper for spelling errors.
- I have used capital letters correctly. (This includes capitals for names of people, places, and things and at the beginning of each sentence.)
- I have used correct punctuation. (This includes using periods, questions marks, and exclamation points at the ends of sentences and using commas and apostrophes when needed.)
- I have checked to see that my work is legible. (Teach this word by telling the students that if they aren't careful, a teacher may not be able to read their work because their *e's* look like *a's* or words or sentences are squeezed together. Using margins and spaces, show the students how a writing or math paper should look.)
- I have said what I meant to say. (Explain that a person who is writing might sometimes mean to write something a certain way, but write something different. For example, you might think you wrote, "The sky is blue" but you really wrote, "The sky blue." Scout wrote, "Dogs can swam" and meant, "Dogs can swim.")
- I have checked to see that each sentence is a whole sentence. (Use this time to review that a whole sentence must have a subject and predicate or a noun and a verb—use terminology students have been taught.)
- I have checked to see that math papers use the correct sign. (Don't assume they are all addition problems, just because the first problem is!)
- I have checked to see that this paper is a sample of my best work! (Remind the students that they should be proud of everything they turn in to their teacher.)

Compliment the students on the great list they compiled.

SONG:

Say:

Let's sing another verse of our song!

Lead the students in singing the next verse of *A School Of Champions!*

School of Champions!/Grade 2
(Sung to *Old MacDonald Had a Farm*)

We are a school of champions—champ, champ, champions!
We check our work, then turn it in—champ, champ, champions!
With a check-check here and a check-check there.
Here a check, there a check,
Everywhere a check-check.
We are a school of champions—champ, champ, champions!

ACTIVITY 2:

Begin the second activity by saying:

I'm going to give you a chance to proofread a paper right now. I have an old paper of Scout's. There are 20 mistakes on this worksheet. Cross out Scout's mistakes and make the correction above the mistake.

Have the students take their folder and a pencil from their desks. Give each student a copy of *Scout's Mistakes*. Have the students correct the paper. When the students have completed the worksheet, review it with the class.

CONCLUSION:

Conclude the lesson by saying:

Well, boys and girls, the study skill you learned today can definitely help you be a champion! If you check your papers for mistakes, I guarantee that you will get better grades! Do you know how I can make a guarantee like that? (If the students find the mistakes, they can correct them before their teacher has a chance to count them wrong.)

Put the worksheet we just did into your *A School Of Champions!* folder. I'm going to give you another picture of Scout to color. Don't color it during work time, because that would not be the behavior of a champion. When you've finished coloring the picture, put it into your folder.

Give each student a copy of *Champions Proofread Their Papers!* Then say:

Next time Scout and I come back, we'll share another study skill that will help you become champion students! Right, Scout? (Have Scout bark one time, then settle down immediately.)

Scout is beginning to act like a champion! Yeah, Scout!

Scout's Mistakes

Name: __scout__

my name is scout

i kan jump.

i can ran

i go to The blue ribon

schol For Dogs

3	5	1	3	7	3
+1	+2	+1	−3	−5	−1
3	7	6	1	2	4

Champions Proofread Their Papers!

LESSON 5 – GRADE 2
Champions Read Directions Carefully

Goal:

The students will learn the importance of reading directions before beginning work and that looking over a completed assignment is a good idea. The students will have an opportunity to practice completing a page of written directions.

Materials Needed:

For the leader:
- ☐ Dog puppet or 4-legged stuffed toy named *Scout*
- ☐ *A School Of Champions! Grade 2* song (optional, page 118)

For each student:
- ☐ *Written Directions Practice* (page 161)
- ☐ *Champions Always Read Directions!* (page 162)
- ☐ *A School Of Champions!* folder
- ☐ Crayons
- ☐ Pencil

Presentation Preparation:

Reproduce *Written Directions Practice* and *Champions Always Read Directions!* for each student. Gather any other necessary materials.

Lesson:

INTRODUCTION:

Introduce the lesson by saying:

Hello, boys and girls! Scout and I are back to teach you another lesson about how to become champion students.

Scout, say *hello* to the boys and girls! (Have Scout bark a couple of times, then get quiet.)

Good girl, Scout! You really are on your way to becoming a champion!

How are all of you doing? Are you keeping fresh in your mind your goal of the champion you want to become? (Allow time for the students to respond.)

Are you trying hard to be good listeners: using your ears, eyes, and mind? (Allow time for the students to respond.)

Are you trying to stay organized? (Allow time for the students to respond.)

Are you proofreading all your papers? (Allow time for the students to respond.)

SONG:

Sing *A School Of Champions!* song. Say:

Let's sing *A School Of Champions!* We know many verses now. Shall we sing them all? (Let the students decide. If they don't like singing, sing only the first verse. If the students like to sing, singing all the verses is a good way to review all the rules they've learned.)

A School Of Champions!/Grade 2
(Sung to *Old MacDonald Had a Farm*)

We are a school of champions—champ, champ, champions!
We work to win and try each day—champ, champ, champions!
With a win-win here and a try-try there.
Here a win, there a try,
Everywhere a win-try.
We are a school of champions—champ, champ, champions!

We are a school of champions—champ, champ, champions!
We listen to our teacher every day—champ, champ, champions!
With a listen-listen here and a listen-listen there.
Here a listen, there a listen,
Everywhere a listen-listen.
We are a school of champions—champ, champ, champions!

We are a school of champions—champ, champ, champions!
And every day we organize—champ, champ, champions!
With a book bag here and folder there.
Here a book bag, there a folder,
Everywhere a book bag, folder.
We are a school of champions—champ, champ, champions!

We are a school of champions—champ, champ, champions!
We check our work, then turn it in—champ, champ, champions!
With a check-check here and a check-check there.
Here a check, there a check,
Everywhere a check-check.
We are a school of champions—champ, champ, champions!

Compliment the students on the great job they did singing the song.

STORY:

Read or tell the following story:

As I told you before, Scout is doing a great job of becoming a champion student at *The Blue Ribbon School For Dogs*. She tries hard every day, she listens, she's organized, and she's been checking all her papers before turning them in. Doing all those things has helped Scout do better in school, and her grades are showing an improvement! Her parents are proud of her. Mr. Beagle, her teacher, is proud of her. And best of all, Scout is proud of herself!

But she still has a few bad habits that are hard to break. One of those bad habits is that Scout never takes time to read the directions on her worksheets. Mr. Beagle frequently reminds his students to read the directions before beginning to work on their papers. He has told the puppies that it's a good practice to look over the whole paper before beginning to work. But no matter how many times he has reminded the class of these good habits, Scout does not take the time to follow her teacher's advice.

It's not that Scout doesn't want to do well, because you *know* she wants to be a champion. But she just doesn't think it's necessary to read directions when she already knows how to do the worksheets and other assignments her teacher gives the class. If there is a question followed by a blank space, she fills it in. If there are two columns, it is usually a matching page. Scout draws lines between the columns to connect two things that go together. If there are math problems, Scout just does them! She doesn't see the sense in bothering to read what she can figure out for herself.

One day last week, Mr. Beagle became very frustrated. He knew Scout never took time to read the directions on assignments, so he decided to teach her a lesson. He created some very special worksheets to show Scout and everyone else in the class that it's important to read directions before beginning an assignment.

The first time Mr. Beagle gave out one of his special worksheets was during a math lesson on addition. When Scout got the worksheet, she couldn't believe how much work Mr. Beagle was assigning. It took her a lo-on-ong time to do the 100 math problems on the page! When she finally finished the worksheet, Scout went to the teacher's desk to turn in her paper. Mr. Beagle looked at the paper and said, "Wow, Scout! You really felt like doing math today! I guess you wanted to get a lot of practice!"

Scout was puzzled. "What do you mean?" she asked. "I did what was assigned."

Mr. Beagle said, "If you had read the directions, you'd know that you were supposed to choose only 10 of the problems to complete."

Scout was so mad at herself! She had done 90 more problems than she was supposed to do!

The second time Mr. Beagle assigned one of his special worksheets was during a science class. There were only 10 questions on the paper. Once again, Scout didn't bother to read the directions. She could tell that it was just a regular worksheet with questions followed by blanks on which she was supposed to write answers.

Scout began the worksheet immediately. The questions were very difficult, but Scout worked hard to do her best. She couldn't believe how hard the worksheet was! Mr. Beagle had never given such a hard worksheet to the class before. Scout was not sure that her answers to many of the questions were correct.

When she finally finished, she went to Mr. Beagle's desk with her worksheet. He looked at it and said, "Scout, you must really want to earn some extra-credit points for your science grade!"

"What do you mean?" asked Scout.

"If you had read the directions," answered Mr. Beagle, "you'd know that this is a sample of the kind of work Grade 3 students do in science. The directions say that you don't have to actually answer the questions. You were just supposed to read the questions so you could get a preview of what you will be learning in Grade 3 science!"

Scout was upset with herself and upset with Mr. Beagle. It seemed like he was trying to fool her. She had worked for more than an hour to complete these questions. And all for nothing!

You might think Scout would have learned her lesson by now. But it took one more of Mr. Beagle's special worksheets to finally teach her that reading directions and looking over an assignment before beginning are important steps.

Mr. Beagle told his students he was giving them a whole sheet of written directions to follow. Scout thought, "Mr. Beagle is not going to fool me this time! I will read the directions at the top of the page."

So Scout read the directions at the top of the page. The directions said: "Read all directions before beginning."

Scout said to herself, "OK, I read the directions. Now I will do the paper."

Every item had a different direction for Scout to follow. On #1, she had to write her name backward. On #2, she was directed to put three words in ABC order. Scout worked hard and was very proud of herself … until she came to #10—the last direction. Item #10 said very clearly, "Do not start this assignment until your teacher says you may begin."

Scout looked up from her paper. Mr. Beagle was looking at her. So was every other puppy in the class. They were waiting for her to find out that she was supposed to read the directions and look over the page before beginning her work!

DISCUSSION:

Ask the students:

Why do you think it's important to read the directions each time you start a new assignment? (You cannot assume all pages are the same. One worksheet's directions may tell you to circle the correct answers. Another may tell you to write out the words, and another may tell you to draw a line under the correct answers. Reading directions will help you in Grade 2 and whenever you have to fill out a paper or a form or complete an assignment.)

Why do you think it's helpful to look over the whole assignment before beginning to work? (If you look over the whole assignment before you begin to work, there will be no surprises. You will get an idea of what you have to do and how much time you will need to complete the assignment.)

Continue the lesson by saying:

Scout was trying to take shortcuts by not reading the directions. I wonder how many of you have ever done the same thing. I won't ask you to raise your hands, but I want you to admit to yourselves if you've ever skipped reading the directions on a worksheet or other assignment.

Scout has learned her lesson. She always reads the directions now and looks over the page before beginning her work. Right, Scout?" (Have Scout bark one time.)

SONG:

Say:

We have a new verse for our song. Sing along with me.

Lead the students in singing the next verse of *A School Of Champions!*

A School Of Champions!/Grade 2
(Sung to *Old MacDonald Had a Farm*)

We are a school of champions—champ, champ, champions!
We read all directions on our work—champ, champ, champions!
With a read–read here, and a read–read there.
Here a read, there a read,
Everywhere a read–read.
We are a school of champions—champ, champ, champions!

Compliment the students on the great job they did singing the song.

ACTIVITY:

Give each student a copy of *Written Directions Practice*. Have the students take out their folder and a pencil. Then say:

We're going to complete the same worksheet Scout had to do. It's a worksheet full of directions. Take your time and read the directions at the top. Look over the rest of the sheet before you begin. Ready, begin! (Allow an appropriate amount of time for the students to complete the worksheet.)

When the allotted time has elapsed, let the students check their own papers while you review the answers. Then instruct the students to put their papers into their folder.

Continue the activity by saying:

Now I'll give you a picture of Scout reading directions. And believe me, she reads all directions now that she has learned her lesson! Please don't color this picture during work time, because that's something a champion wouldn't do. When you've finished coloring, be sure to add this picture to your *A School Of Champions!* folder. (Give each student a copy of *Champions Always Read Directions!* If the teacher prefers, give the stack of papers to him/her to distribute at a later time.)

CONCLUSION:

Conclude the lesson by saying:

Boys and girls, it's time for Scout and me to leave. Remember that we've learned another very important study skill that will help you all become champion students. What is the skill we learned today? (Always take time to read the directions and look over the assignment before beginning your work.)

Our next visit will be Scout's last visit to your classroom. She'll go back to being a full-time champion student at *The Blue Ribbon School For Dogs*, and each of you will be a champion student at _____ School!

Scout, say *goodbye* to the boys and girls! (Have Scout bark one time.) **I am so proud of this puppy!**

Optional: Sing any or all of *A School Of Champions!*

Written Directions Practice

Name _____

Directions: Read all the directions before beginning.

1. Write your name backward on this line:

   _____

2. Write these words in ABC order: mouse, cat, dog.

   _____

3. If today is Tuesday, draw 3 stars on the line.
   If today is not Tuesday, draw 1 star.

   _____

4. Write the 5 numbers that come after 2 when you are counting. Circle the 4.

   _____

5. Put an X on the number 3 in the answer you just wrote.

6. Draw a triangle and draw a circle in the middle of the triangle.

7. Draw a cat in the right margin of this paper.

8. On this line, write the letter that begins your last name. Circle this letter. _____

9. Write an addition problem on the line. Do not write the answer.

   _____

10. Answer any 6 questions on this worksheet.

Champions Always Read Directions And Look Over The Page Before Beginning An Assignment!

Champions Have Good Test-Taking Skills!

Goal:

The students will learn why teachers give tests and will be given tips that will help them do well on future tests. This lesson will address test-taking tips on topics such as having a good test-taking attitude, how to handle test anxiety, the importance of using time wisely, and the importance of reading all test directions and questions. The students will learn how to study and prepare for a test and will be given practice in the form of a multiple choice test on study skills.

Materials Needed:

For the leader:
- ☐ Dog puppet or 4-legged stuffed toy named *Scout*
- ☐ *A School Of Champions! Grade 2* song (optional, page 118)
- ☐ Chalkboard and chalk or whiteboard and marker
- ☐ Posterboard
- ☐ Marker

For each student:
- ☐ *A School Of Champions!* folder
- ☐ *Test For Champions* (pages 172-173)
- ☐ *Champions Use Good Test-Taking Skills!* (page 174)
- ☐ *Certificate* (page 175)
- ☐ Crayons
- ☐ Paper
- ☐ Pencil

Presentation Preparation:

Reproduce *Test For Champions*, *Champions Use Good Test-Taking Skills!*, and *Certificate* for each student. Fill out the *Certificates* or have the students write their own name on the line provided. Gather any other necessary materials.

Lesson:

INTRODUCTION:

Introduce the last lesson by saying:

> Boy and girls, Scout and I are back today to teach you one last lesson that will help you become part of *A School Of Champions!* at _____ School.
>
> For the past five lessons, we've been teaching you study skills that will help you do a good job at school. I hope you've been learning and trying as hard as Scout has been trying. She's doing very well at *The Blue Ribbon School For Dogs!* Right, Scout? (Have Scout bark one time, then sit quietly.)
>
> You are such a well-behaved puppy!

SONG:

Say:

> Let's review what you've learned from the past five lessons. We'll do this review by singing! Let's sing all the verses of our song.

A School Of Champions!/Grade 2
(Sung to *Old MacDonald Had a Farm*)

We are a school of champions—champ, champ, champions!
We work to win and try each day—champ, champ, champions!
With a win-win here and a try-try there.
Here a win, there a try,
Everywhere a win-try.
We are a school of champions—champ, champ, champions!

We are a school of champions—champ, champ, champions!
We listen to our teacher every day—champ, champ, champions!
With a listen-listen here and a listen-listen there.
Here a listen, there a listen,
Everywhere a listen-listen.
We are a school of champions—champ, champ, champions!

We are a school of champions—champ, champ, champions!
And every day we organize—champ, champ, champions!
With a book bag here and a folder there.
Here a book bag, there a folder,
Everywhere a book bag-folder.
We are a school of champions—champ, champ, champions!

We are a school of champions—champ, champ, champions!
We check our work, then turn it in—champ, champ, champions!
With a check-check here and a check-check there.
Here a check, there a check,
Everywhere a check-check.
We are a school of champions—champ, champ, champions!

We are a school of champions—champ, champ, champions!
We read all directions on our work—champ, champ, champions!
With a read–read here, and a read–read there.
Here a read, there a read,
Everywhere a read–read.
We are a school of champions—champ, champ, champions!

Then say:

Great job! And are you doing all these things to help yourselves become champions in school? (Allow time for students' answers. If the classroom teacher is in the room, ask for his/her input.)

STORY:

Read or tell the following story:

I want you to know that Scout has been doing a fantastic job at *The Blue Ribbon School For Dogs*! She doesn't need as many reminders as she used to, as you can probably tell from her behavior in this class. She is still a playful puppy, but she knows that during recess, after school, and weekends are the best times for playing.

Mr. Beagle is very happy with the progress Scout has made. He feels that Scout and all the puppies in his class are doing a great job of learning Grade 2 subjects.

One day last week, Mr. Beagle told his class that he wanted to see how much they had actually learned. He told them the best way he could measure the progress they have made was to give them a test.

When Mr. Beagle said those words, Scout got nervous. In fact, she feels her heart beat a little faster whenever Mr. Beagle says *test*.

Since Mr. Beagle had taught Scout so many study skills that have helped her do well in school, she decided to talk with him about her feelings about tests. She thought that maybe he could give her a few good test-taking tips. So at recess time, when the other puppies went out to play, Scout stayed behind to talk with Mr. Beagle about her feelings about tests.

"Mr. Beagle, I always get nervous when you talk about giving us a test," said Scout.

Mr. Beagle said, "That's great! Being nervous is not always a bad way to feel!"

"What do you mean?" asked Scout.

"Of course, I don't want you to be so nervous that you can't think," said Mr. Beagle, "but a little nervousness means you care about how you do on tests."

"I *do* care!" said Scout.

"So use that nervous energy to do your best!" said Mr. Beagle. "Just like an actor who is going on stage or an athlete who is getting ready for a competition. A little nervousness can actually help your performance!"

Mr. Beagle told Scout that if she would take a few deep breaths and say some positive statements to herself, her nervousness could be changed to confident energy … especially if she was prepared for the test.

"How should I get prepared?" asked Scout.

"You do exactly what you have been doing, Scout! Do your work, keep up with your assignments, use good study skills, and review the material before the test."

Then Mr. Beagle told Scout that she should go out and play with the other puppies and that the whole class would discuss this important subject after recess.

Scout ran outside and played with the other puppies in her class. It was a beautiful day, and Scout felt great. Scout loves to play! But the game was not the real reason Scout felt so good. She felt proud and happy because she knows she is a champion!

DISCUSSION:

Ask the students:

What do you think Mr. Beagle meant when he said that being a little nervous can help a person do better on a test? (If students aren't at all nervous, it might show that they don't care how they do on the test.)

Stand and demonstrate how nervousness can be changed to positive energy. Show this by saying what a baseball player might be thinking as he approaches the plate. Say:

"I hope I do a good job for the team. I'm going to take a deep breath and do my best." Thinking positive thoughts such as these will help change nervousness to excitement! That feeling can actually help a person do well.

Mr. Beagle talked with the puppies about what they could do to prepare for a test. Let's take the time to have the same discussion. Here are some tips that might help you do well when it's time for you to take a test.

Write *Tips For Tests* at the top of the posterboard. Then present the following tips by leading a discussion and having the students come up with some of the ideas listed. Do this by asking leading questions such as, "What can you do the night before a test?" Questions such as these will help the students think about the ideas on this list. (Below is the list of questions followed by appropriate student answers to record on the *Tips For Tests* chart. The completed chart should be left in the classroom.) Ask the students:

How can your thoughts about a test help you do well? (A good attitude and positive thinking help. Be confident and tell yourself that you are a smart person who will do his or her best!)

What can you do the night before that will help you do well on a test? (Get enough sleep so your brain is rested. This is good practice on a night before a test and every school night!)

What can you do at home before you come to school that will help you do well on a test? (Eat a healthy breakfast. If you don't put "fuel" into your body, you won't have the energy to think clearly.)

How can your attendance affect how well you do on tests? (Missing school will have a big impact on how well you do on tests, as well as on regular assignments. Teachers try to help students who have missed school be up to date, but students who are absent miss lots of information.)

What study skill about directions did Scout learn last week? How would that skill apply to taking tests? (Read the directions on a test paper. If you are supposed to circle something, don't underline! If you're supposed to write the answer using whole sentences, a teacher might count your answer wrong if you write only one or two words.)

What about a multiple choice test with several answer choices for every question? Can anyone think of a tip that might help you on that kind of test? (If more leading is needed, ask: "Should you choose the first answer if it seems like a good one?" If you're taking a multiple choice test, read all the answers. The first answer might look pretty good, but maybe the last answer is the best one.)

How can time help you or hurt you on a test? What would be a good rule about how time should be used? (Use your time wisely. Don't spend too much time on any question. If you work for 20 minutes on Question #1, you may not have time to answer the rest of the questions.)

If you are taking a regular classroom test on spelling words or math or science, what can you do ahead of time that will help you know the information? (Study, study, study! While you cannot study for aptitude tests or "normed" achievement tests, you can certainly study for regular tests that your teacher may give.)

If the students are getting ready to take an achievement test, discuss:

- Preparing for an achievement test by following the good test-taking skills listed on the chart
- Using a #2 pencil when taking a test that will be graded by a machine
- The importance of using time wisely when taking a timed test
- Tips on how to use an answer sheet
- Keeping the test paper free of stray marks
- Checking a separate answer sheet to make sure the numbered answer blank corresponds to the question number
- Filling answer bubbles in completely, thoroughly erasing any changed answers

Explain that the students may not know the answer to every question on an achievement test. Test preparers often include material from higher grade levels so they can see how much a Grade 2 student actually knows!

ACTIVITY 1:

Give each student a piece of paper. Have the students take out their folder and a pencil. Then say:

Let's talk for a moment about a good way to study when you'll be taking a classroom test.

Let's pretend your teacher gave you a list of words to learn to spell. Here is a difficult word to learn. (Write the word *chocolate* on the board.)

How would you try to learn to spell this word? (Students might suggest writing the word 10 times or having someone quiz them.)

The problem with writing a word over and over is that you may not be thinking about what you're writing. So writing the word over and over will not help you learn to spell it. You could write a word 100 times and still not know how to spell it if your hand is doing all the work and your brain is thinking about lunch! And having someone quiz you won't help until you have done something to make the word stick in your brain. (Point to the word *chocolate*, which you've written on the board.)

My suggestion is that you study *with thought!* Look at the word closely, then break it into parts. Look at *chocolate.* It has three parts – *choc – o – late.* Look at how to spell choc – the *ch* makes the regular sound. *C-h-o-c Choc.* Then there is an *o* by itself. Then there is the word *late.* So the word is really *choc - o - late.* Look at the word again and think about that. (Erase the word *chocolate*.)

Now write the word *chocolate* on your paper. (Most students will be able to spell the word correctly. If they cannot, spend a little more time going over the word.)

***Chocolate* is a difficult word to spell, and you just learned it in a minute! Being quiet and thinking about what you're supposed to learn is the best tip I can give you.**

Let's try one more word. (Write the word *too* on the board.)

This is not a hard word to spell, but many people mix up which *too* to use in different situations. Let's talk about that. This word *too* is used when there is too much of something. I always think to myself, "There are too many *o's* in this word. So the spelling of the *too* that means *too much* has extra *o's!"* How do you spell the other words that sound like *too?* (Review the spellings and meanings of *to* and *two*. Most children realize that *two* is the number, so spend time talking about the fact that if you're going to the store, or reading to your sister, you need only one *o* in the word. Then quiz the students by saying several sentences incorporating the words *to*, *too*, and *two*. As you say each sentence aloud, ask the students to choose which spelling is correct, then write their answers on the paper.)

We just spent a few seconds on these words, and now you'll always know which one to use! You must always take time to quietly think about the material your test will cover.

SONG:

Lead the students in singing the last verse of *A School Of Champions!* Say:

Let's sing the last verse of *A School Of Champions!*

School of Champions!/Grade 2
(Sung to *Old MacDonald Had a Farm*)

We are a school of champions—champ, champ, champions!
We study and prepare before all tests—champ, champ, champions!
With a study–study here and a test–test there.
Here a study, there a test,
Everywhere a study–test.
We are a school of champions—champ, champ, champions!

A School Of Champions! © 2007 Mar★co Products, Inc. 1.800.448.2197

Then say:

> **Great job! Now we're going to take a little test!** (If the students groan, remind them that a positive attitude is helpful.)

ACTIVITY 2:

Administer the *Test For Champions*. Depending on the students' reading level, you may want to read the questions and answers aloud. When the students have completed the test, review the answers orally with the class. Allow the students to check their own papers. The purpose of the test is not to take grades, but to give the students one final review.

CONCLUSION:

Conclude the final lesson by saying:

> **Congratulations, boys and girls! You have done it! You are now a part of *A School Of Champions!* at _____ School. I'm proud of you, and I hope you're proud of yourselves!**

> **I have a *Certificate* for each of you.**

Call up the students one by one and hand each one a *Certificate* with his/her name on it. Shake hands with each child or have Scout shake hands. Then say:

> **I have one last picture of Scout to give you. Don't color it during work time, because that's not something a champion would do. When you have finished coloring this picture, you may put it into your *A School Of Champions!* folder. This is our last lesson, so you may take that folder home today.** (Give each student a copy of *Champions Use Good Test-Taking Skills!*)

> **Tell your parents all about Scout and what you have learned. Tell them that you and Scout are now part of *A School Of Champions!***

> **Let's give a silent cheer.** (Have the students cheer silently.)

> **Scout won't be coming back to this class because she has done her job here. She'll go back to being a full-time student at *The Blue Ribbon School For Dogs*.**

> **Scout, do you have something to say to these boys and girls?** (Have Scout bark one time.)

> **That's puppy talk for, "We are champions!"**

Let's sing the first verse of our song one more time!

A School Of Champions!/Grade 2
(Sung to *Old MacDonald Had a Farm*)

We are a school of champions—champ, champ, champions!
We work to win and try each day—champ, champ, champions!
With a win-win here and a try-try there.
Here a win, there a try,
Everywhere a win-try.
We are a school of champions—champ, champ, champions!

171

Test For Champions

Name _____

Directions: Read the questions and all the answers below. Choose the best answer for each question and make an **✗** in the box alongside the answer.

1. A champion must think positively and make a picture in his/her head. A good picture would be:

- ☐ the person getting an *F* on a paper.
- ☐ the person getting picked on by other students.
- ☐ the person standing proudly in the future.
- ☐ the person losing his/her papers.

2. When you listen, you should:

- ☐ keep your body still.
- ☐ keep your eyes on the speaker.
- ☐ keep your mind on what the speaker is saying.
- ☐ All of these are important.

3. When you listen to the teacher's directions, you should:

- ☐ listen to only half of what the teacher says.
- ☐ listen to all the directions.
- ☐ not listen at all.
- ☐ talk.

4. Keeping your desk organized will:

- ☐ help you get straight *A's*.
- ☐ help you know where everything is.
- ☐ make you a better friend.
- ☐ keep you healthy.

5 Before you turn in a homework paper, you should:

- ☐ proofread it.
- ☐ tear it up.
- ☐ erase your name.
- ☐ drop it in a puddle.

6 To make sure you're doing your work correctly, you should:

- ☐ copy from your neighbor's papers.
- ☐ ask your older brothers or sisters.
- ☐ read the directions carefully.
- ☐ drop it in a puddle.

7 When you study, you can remember more if you:

- ☐ study in front of the TV.
- ☐ study while you're eating dinner.
- ☐ write the answer 53 times.
- ☐ think about the material you're trying to learn.

8 Students take tests because:

- ☐ tests show what students have learned.
- ☐ teachers are mean.
- ☐ the principal said they have to.
- ☐ there is no reason.

9 To be a champion student, you should:

- ☐ think positive thoughts.
- ☐ listen to the teacher.
- ☐ organize your desk and materials.
- ☐ proofread all work before turning it in.
- ☐ read all directions on assignments and tests.
- ☐ study by quietly thinking about the information.
- ☐ All of the above!

Champions Use Good Test-Taking Skills!

_____'s
SCHOOL NAME

School Of Champions!

_____
NAME OF STUDENT

has completed the
Grade 2 program
for
A School Of Champions!

_____
SIGNATURE

_____
DATE

About The Author

Rosanne Sheritz Sartori was a classroom teacher and elementary counselor for 30 years. Toward the end of her career as an educator, she began her career as an author of guidance material. Her first two books, *Lively Lessons for Classroom Sessions* and *More Lively Lessons for Classroom Sessions,* are used by educators throughout the world. Other published works include, *Stand Up Against Bullies for K-2, Stand Up Against Bullies for Grades 3-5, Tales of Temper, A New Start: One Child's Struggle with Obesity*, and *Colorful Counseling*.

Rosanne lives with her husband, Glenn, in St. Louis, Missouri and is constantly busy. Besides writing, she presents her ideas at educational conferences, does volunteer work, makes jewelry, teaches art, and lives each day to the fullest. She believes that *enthusiasm* is the key to a full life.